D1221991

Abel Buell of Connecticut

Abel Buell
OF CONNECTICUT

Silversmith
Type Founder & Engraver

BY LAWRENCE C. WROTH

Middletown
Wesleyan University Press
1958

First published in a limited edition
of 102 copies as the Fifteenth Publication
of the Acorn Club of Connecticut in 1926;
now completely revised and enlarged.

The device on the title page is adapted from a silversmith's mark presumed to be that of Abel Buell.

Library of Congress Catalog Card Number: 58-13601

Composed and printed in the United States of America
Second edition revised; first printing

This essay in American antiquarianism
is dedicated in its revised form
to my fellow members,
past, present, and future,
of the Walpole Society

Contents

Illustrations

Preface to the Second Edition

ON a later page of this book it is remarked that Abel Buell was fortunate in the number of second chances which life held out to him. His biographer has been similarly favored. The Wesleyan University Press has given me a second chance by proposing the publication of a new and revised edition of *Abel Buell of Connecticut: Silversmith, Type Founder & Engraver,* originally brought out by the Acorn Club in 1926. I am grateful for the opportunity thus provided to present new material and to restate certain interpretations which later discoveries have shown to be incorrect. These additions and revisions are the result of my own continuing interest in the subject stimulated by new data generously conveyed to me by Mr. Thompson R. Harlow, Librarian of the Connecticut Historical Society; Mr. Clarence S. Brigham, Director of the American Antiquarian Society; and Mr. Robert W. G. Vail, Director of the New York Historical Society. More specific acknowledgment to these and others is made in the ensuing text and notes. I am grateful also to Mr. Harold Hugo of the Meriden Gravure Company for aid in connection with the illustrations which, as always in his association with authors and publishers, has gone far beyond the actual production of the engravings. I owe particular thanks to Miss Marion W. Adams, my former associate in the work of the John Carter Brown Library, for editorial assistance and for advice of the sort which has been of singular helpfulness to me throughout the years. Finally, I record my thanks to the members of the Acorn Club of Connecticut for their willingness to permit a new edition of the book which, thirty-two years ago, designed by my friend Carl Purington Rollins, they issued as their fifteenth publication.

L. C. W.

Providence, Rhode Island
May 1, 1958

Preface to the First Edition

THE biographical sketch of Abel Buell presented here through the medium of the Acorn Club had its origin in an admission of ignorance that I was compelled to make to Mr. George S. Godard at a session some three years ago of the Bibliographical Society of America. It was in the city of New Haven itself that the ironic lords of human destiny permitted me to discourse on early American type founding without mentioning the Buell experiment conducted in the year 1769 within a few miles of where I stood while saying my piece. To Mr. Godard's "What about Abel Buell?" I could only reply that the little I knew was contained in a footnote to my paper. Thereupon began my first instruction in the achievement of Abel Buell as a type founder. The interest then aroused in me by the Connecticut State Librarian has resulted after many months in the book now before the reader.

Throughout the course of this study I have been particularly fortunate in my correspondents. Mr. Godard not only started me on this quest, but since that beginning he has helped me to further it in every possible way. I owe him thanks in particular for searching out and copying for me many documents preserved in the Connecticut State Archives. Mr. Albert Carlos Bates of the Connecticut Historical Society has guided me aright many times when without his help I would have gone astray because of my lack of any considerable body of Connecticut lore. Mr. Andrew Keogh has searched the unpublished portion of the Stiles Papers in the Yale University Library with happy results for the ensuing account of Buell's type founding venture. Mr. William Fowler Hopson has given me encouragement and practical assistance, not the least valuable feature of which was to put me in communication with Mr. Donald Lines Jacobus, the New Haven editor and genealogist. Mr. John K. Wright of the American Geographical Society has sent me a photographic copy of the Buell Map of the United States, a cartographical document of which one of the few known copies is found in the collection which he administers. Miss Margaret Bingham Stillwell of the Annmary Brown Memorial, Mr. Clarence S. Brigham of the American Antiquarian Society, Mr. Alexander J. Wall of the New York Historical Society, Mr. Wilberforce Eames of the New York Public Library, Mr. George Parker Winship of the Widener Memorial Library, and Mr. Howard Miller Chapin of the Rhode Island Historical Society have been helpful by suggestion or by the contribution of information. Mrs. George Munson Curtis has given me permission to photograph the four silver cups, now in her collection, that Buell made in 1797 for the North Haven Congregational Church. For aid in other particulars, I wish to thank the assistants of those librarians whose names have been mentioned, as well as the several officials and attendants of the Library of Congress and of the John Hay Library of Brown University to whom I have appealed in times of need. To the staff of the John Carter Brown Library I have already expressed my feeling of obligation for service cheerfully rendered.

L. C. W.

The John Carter Brown Library
Providence, March 30, 1926

Abel Buell of Connecticut

Silversmith, Engraver, Type Founder & Inventor

IT should be understood that this story of the life of Abel Buell is not intended for readers who have lived always in large cities. Only small town denizens will be able to visualize Abel Buell or wholly to appreciate him. Only they can see him hurrying along the main street with eager, unsatisfied eyes and muttering lips. They alone can remember being buttonholed by him to be told about his patent corn planter, or to be talked into buying stock in his new mill, or perhaps simply to be informed of incipient inventions that would bring ease to those who labor and gold to the restless palms of the inventor. This sort of man is seen only in small towns. When he moves to a metropolis he is lost in the dun throng that reads the Patent Office Gazette in the public library, or else he shaves and starches himself and becomes a company promoter equally without distinctive characteristics. He is a type imperfectly set apart in the minds of city dwellers, and these will be tired by the simple annals of his life. This much having been said in warning to those who propose reading the story, it only remains to proceed with its relation.

The versatile Abel Buell, if I may use that worn epithet of description once and then have done with it, was born in Killingworth, Connecticut, on February 1, 1742. His father was John Buell of Killingworth, the fourth in descent from William Buell of Chesterton, Huntingdonshire, England, and Windsor, Connecticut.[1] At the usual age, the boy was apprenticed to Ebenezer Chittenden, a goldsmith of East Guilford, now Madison, Connecticut, and later of

New Haven, with whom he was to be associated in one way or another for many years after the expiration of his term of indenture.[2] His professional career was not a happy one. It began in disgrace and ended in defeat, but though disappointment and frustration became the commonplace experiences of his life, Buell yet was able to conduct himself so as to be remembered willingly by the generations that followed him.

Late in the year 1762, at the age of twenty or twenty-one, Buell, his apprenticeship concluded, established himself independently in Killingworth as a goldsmith. It was at this time also that he was married to the first of his four successive wives. The author of the Buell family genealogy suggests that the maiden name of this lady was Mary Parker, but another authority of equal weight makes clear by implication that in this marriage we have enacted before us the age-old Dick Whittington drama in which the industrious apprentice marries into the master's family. Coming to the specific instance we learn that Mary Buell was born Mary Chittenden, sister of Ebenezer Chittenden, the accomplished silversmith to whom the young husband had been articled.[3] Mary Chittenden's maternal uncle was the Reverend Samuel Johnson, first president of King's College, now Columbia University, and the "father of Episcopacy in Connecticut." One of her brothers was Thomas Chittenden who in 1778 became the first governor of Vermont. The closeness of the association between Buell and Mary Chittenden's brother, Ebenezer, the silversmith, will reveal itself as the story of his life proceeds. It is especially to be observed in the present connection that when, in 1775, a New Haven constable attached for debt the entirety of Buell's estate, his dwelling was described as the eastern half of the house "belonging to the Defendant & Ebenezer Chittenden." These words indicate a closer relationship between the two families than that of simple friendship.

The probabilities are strongly in support of the Chittenden origin of Mrs. Mary Buell.

DISASTER

The future would have looked bright enough to most young men beginning adult life with a trade, a small inherited property of his own,[4] and a well-connected, not impecunious bride as shields against the world's indifference. For Abel Buell, however, these did not suffice. I wish I could read his character well enough to know whether it was his restless disposition, his dreams and his impatience, or whether it was mere cupidity that now led him headlong into the error that affected his whole life. Applying his skill in the use of delicate tools to the paper currency of the colony, he succeeded only too well in altering a number of two shillings six pence bills to the more comfortable denomination of thirty shillings. Detected in this offense, he was brought before the Superior Court at Norwich and there on the fourth Tuesday of March, 1764, condemned to be imprisoned and to be cropped of one ear and branded on the forehead with the letter "C."[5] In accordance with another provision of the law, his property was ordered to be sold at the same time to reimburse the holders of his ill-conceived private issue of bills of credit.[6]

Buell's youth at the time of this indiscretion seems to have aroused a general commiseration for his plight. It is said that the brand was placed so high on his forehead as to be concealed by his hair, and that in carrying out the sentence of mutilation the jailers cropped only the tip of his ear and then replaced the bit of flesh so quickly that the wounded member suffered little disfigurement.[7] In the other particulars of his sentence, however, the same leniency was not observed. He was duly carried to the New London prison and his forfeited property was sent to the auctioneer's block.

It is unprofitable to attempt the condonation of an ancient crime. In the case of Buell's transgression, however, one is permitted to reflect upon the shrewdness of the temptation that presented itself to a craftsman skilled in the use of pen and graver when a paper note of the rude and ugly colonial fabrication came into his hands. The ease of forging or of altering these bills was a commonplace of knowledge in colonial America. The statute books of the colonies are filled with laws for the punishment of a crime that ceased to threaten the peace of mind of the community only when, in a later century, improved methods of paper manufacture had made the danger much less a matter of concern to the average citizen. An advertisement in a colonial newspaper of the year 1738[8] clearly reflects this abiding apprehension of the earlier period. A convict servant, described as "a very sly artful Fellow" and a "Jack of all Trades" especially skilled in forgery, ran away from Alexander Spotswood of Virginia, and the notice in the Williamsburg paper in which his defection was advertised bore the significant caption "A Caution to the Paper-Money Colonies."

It was not only the criminal forger, however, who was found guilty of offenses against the paper currency. Several respectable engravers among Buell's contemporaries are known to have fallen before the potency of the temptation offered by these crude paper notes. The case of Henry Dawkins, imprisoned on a charge of counterfeiting bills of credit in 1776 has provided us with a document as curious as any in the long history of prisons and prisoners, for so despondent did this misguided engraver become in his crowded cell that he petitioned the New York Committee of Safety to inflict upon him the death penalty "in what manner the honourable House may see fit."[9] Joseph Billings and Richard Brunton turned their gravers to the more quickly rewarded task of counterfeiting and suffered in reputation for their futile ingenuity.[10] The history of forgery here and in other lands so abounds in similar cases that one may think of counterfeiting as the traditional weakness of engravers and, like the Connecticut Assembly, give to young Abel Buell the benefit of a lenient judgment for his youthful infraction of the law.

REHABILITATION

Buell was not the sort of person who remains quiet anywhere, even in imprisonment. When the Assembly met in May, 1764, the young goldsmith's petition for pardon was presented to it for consideration. The delegates were moved to a favorable judgment, and acting, as Buell later reminded them, "from a compassionate regard and pity on his youthful follies," they ordered his release from jail on condition that he procure sureties for good behavior and that he remain within the town of Killingworth unless permitted to pass its limits by special license of the Assembly.[11] Grateful for this much, but irked by the restriction on his movements, Buell presented the following petition to the Assembly of October, 1765:[12]

To the Honourable General Assembly of the Colony of Connecticut now sitting at New haven—

The Memorial of Abel Buell of Killingworth in New-london County Humbly Sheweth that at a Super^r Court Holden at Norwich on ye 4th Tuesday of March AD 1764 Your Honours Memorialist was Legaly & Justly Convicted of the heinous Crime of Altering Sundry of the Bills of Publick Credit of this Colony and suffer^d the Corporal Punishment by Law to be Inflicted on such offenders and continued in Goal [*sic*] untill the Sitting of ye Honor^bl Assembly in May AD 1764 (all which your Honour^s Memorialist acknowledges is Just and Righteous)—

At which Assembly Your Honours in Your Great Wisdom and Goodness was Please to Grant to Your Honours Memorialist Some Enlargement on his Giveing Bond with Surties in the

Penal sum of £100: 0: 0 Conditioned that he Shuld be of Good behaviour and Not Depart the Town of Killingworth without the Special Licenc of this Assembly—

Whereupon Your Honours Memorialist asks Leave Humbly to Represent to Your Honours that on procuring such Bond he was Releas^{d} from Goal [*sic*] and Repair^{d} Immediately to S^{d} Town of Killingworth and hath there Continued Ever sin[c]e according to ye Condition of S^{d} Bond. and always Retaining Gratefull sentiments of Your Honours Goodness hath Endeavour^{d} by Industry and Regular liveing to Render himselfe a Good & profitable Member of Society, and Your honours Memorialist asks leave further to Represent to Your Honours that he is Humbly of oppinion that by being Confind to S^{d} Town of Killingworth he is Under many Disadvantages With Respect to the Maintainanc & Support of himselfe and family and y^{t} by further Enlargement he might be Rendred a more profitable Member of Society. Wherefore, Your Hon^{rs} Memorialist humbly Prays that Your Honours Would take his Case into your Wise Consideration (and if it may be Consistant with the Honour of this Assembly, the Laws of ye Colony, & for ye Good of Society, that Your Honours Would Grant to Your Memorialist Licenc to Trade & Deal without being Subject to the Penalty of the Law, and Release him from his Confinment to the S^{d} Town of Killingworth, Under such Regulation as Your Hon^{rs} in Your Wisdom Shall see fit. And Your Hon^{rs} Memorialist as in Duty Bound Shall Ever Pray

ABEL BUELL

Killingworth October 9th AD 1765

Accompanying this document was an affirmation by the selectmen of Killingworth that the foregoing assertion of good conduct was truly stated by the petitioner, but in this instance neither Buell's plea nor the testimonial of his neighbors availed him. Both houses of Assembly rejected his petition and he was compelled to remain within the confines of Killingworth for another year.

In October, 1766, Buell made a new demand on the

pardoning power of the legislature, and this time his petition was supported by a strong claim for consideration. He represented that in his efforts to deserve the past clemency of the Assembly, he had worked diligently at the perfection of a machine for cutting and polishing crystals and precious stones. The evidence he presented of success in this invention so impressed the delegates that upon giving bond to the amount of £200, he was restored to liberty of movement and to his full privilege of citizenship.[13] Free once more but without property and with the stigma of misconduct upon him, Buell faced the world with only his youth and his active brain and skillful hands as weapons against its inertia and unfriendliness.

For several years following his enlargement from Killingworth and his restoration to civic privileges, Buell applied himself sedulously to the practice of the crafts by which he is best remembered. He seems to have made a serious effort at rehabilitation through the employment of his first recorded invention, the machine for cutting and polishing precious and semi-precious stones which in 1766 had convinced the Connecticut legislature of his worthiness. Something over a year after the ban upon his movements had been rescinded we find him—"Jeweller and Lapidar"—temporarily in Boston advertising his skill and special methods in the preparation of crystals and precious stones. The suggestion which one derives from this advertisement of 1767, presented in full in our chapter "Jeweller & Silversmith," is that he had taken to the roads, had become one of the innumerable ambulatory merchants and craftsmen who carried their wares and their skills from town to town along the highways of colonial America. His Boston advertisement provides the first indication of the foot-loose restlessness which was to characterize his later life.

It was in these years also that he began and consummated the experiments in the making of printing type which, more than anything else, have secured him a place in the crowded memories of his countrymen. His services as a type founder will be related fully in a later section; in this outline of his life, it need only be said that in the month of October, 1769, the Assembly voted him a loan for the purpose of forwarding his achievement of that important craft. It was doubtless because New Haven offered a better field for the establishment of a type foundry that he removed from Killingworth to that town sometime in the year 1770. We can be fairly sure of this date because in a printed petition to the Assembly of October, 1769, he described himself as a resident of Killingworth, while in its issue of September 21, 1770, the *Connecticut Journal* of New Haven, in a notice of the death of his wife Mary, spoke of him as "Mr. Abel Buell, of this town." After this year we must think of him as Abel Buell of New Haven, a craftsman of such skill and of such fertility in ideas that an offended state has taken him back into favor and set him on the road to distinction. Before he shall attain the relative prosperity of his middle years, however, we are to see him struck down for the second time and driven into a long exile from home and family.

At this time then, about the year 1770, we have heard of Buell as one skilled in the trades of silversmith, jeweller, lapidary, and type founder. It was not long after this that he added another accomplishment to his list, for it was in the early years of his New Haven residence that he began to exercise his nimble fingers in the art of copperplate engraving. He engraved a chart of the entrance to the Connecticut River in the year 1773 or 1774; he engraved diplomas for Yale College as early as 1774; and for ten years following he is known to have made use of the burin to such an extent as to necessitate in this story of his career a separate treatment of that phase of his varied activity. In spite of these many irons, or perhaps because of this very element of variety in his interests, Buell could not make things go to his satisfaction. His type foundry, subsidized by the colony, failed at this time to make a beginning as a commercial enterprise; his work as silversmith, jeweller, and lapidary has left small record of achievement; and his employment as engraver clearly was not sufficiently great to ensure him a living. We may conclude that in spite of much and varied activity in the years from 1766 to 1774, the relatively quiet years between his major disasters, he gained little more than a living, certainly nothing in terms of material wealth. Toward the end of the period misfortune again showed him its face.

FRESH CATASTROPHE

The extent and reality of Buell's fresh catastrophe are made explicit in the writ of attachment against his estate procured in the New Haven County Court by the New York printer, James Rivington, under date of February 11, 1775. Our only definite knowledge of the existence of an association with Rivington of such importance as this action indicates is found in an examination of the delightful engraving, later to be more fully discussed, *The Sequel of Arts and Sciences,* the imprint of which reads: "Printed for & Sold by the Proprietors A. B. and J. R. in New-Haven." This was a work, it is believed, of the year 1774, and it may be that its joint publication by Buell and Rivington accounts to some degree for the indebtedness of the one to the other. At any rate in his application for the writ, "James Rivington of the City & Province of New York Merchant" asked that the goods or estate of Buell be attached to the amount of 1000 pounds, York money, to cover indebtedness amounting to 500 pounds in the same currency. In accordance with the prescribed form Rivington averred that he had his book showing the indebtedness "ready in Court to be produced." The plea was granted by John Whiting, justice of the peace. The writ was turned over for execution to John Lathrop, Constable, who on February 13th, made his return in these words:

"Then by Virtue of the within Attachment I attached one half a Dwelling House situate on the Church land on the right side of the Green in S^d New Haven belonging to the Deft. & Ebenezer Chittenden that is to say I attached the East part of S^d House to wit, one half thereof as belonging to the Deft by Order of the Plaintiffs Attorney . . ."

The constable's return goes on with a list of household goods and jewelry stock attached at the same time. The circumstance that the other half of the house was occupied by Ebenezer Chittenden encourages us to hope that some part of the Buell household equipment and a remnant at least of the jewelry stock, were moved next door before the descent of the constable. In a later section we list as interesting from many standpoints the articles in house and shop attached in this melancholy proceeding.[14]

If Rivington was realistic enough to describe Buell in his writ as an "absconded" debtor, Mrs. Buell had even harder names for Rivington in the following notice, dated February 21, 1775, published by her in the *Connecticut Journal* for March 1st of that year:

ALL persons indebted to Mr. Abel Buell, are hereby desired forthwith to settle their accounts with cash, as he has left strict orders with me to put those in suit that are not paid in six weeks after his departure, which orders I am determined to comply with literally and without regard to persons.

And whereas Mr. Rivington of New York, has proceeded to the extraordinary step of attaching our house and every thing in it, without any previous request of me to pay him, which attachment has been followed by a few others, from uneasy persons, for paltry sums even of shillings. I therefore request all creditors, if any there be (though I know of none, and believe there are none of any note, besides the government) to suspend their apprehensions a little while, and set aside their fears.

And as Mr. Buell has lately been blamed for carrying away some debtors of evil note, I request the favour of everyone, not to be too hasty of belief: I hope it is not true; but as all men's characters that are calumniated, require some immediate proof in their favour, and perhaps Mr. Buell's on some accounts especially, I hereby notify to all his creditors, or even to any indifferent persons who choose to see it, that I can with very little trouble, (by stubborn facts, in the shape of Rivington's own figures, letters, invoices and receipts) prove that Mr. Buell owes him only £175 lawful, and tho' Mr. Buell has not left me cash, yet I am in possession of enough to pay that sum thrice over; and further I can shew, that Mr. Buell has done Rivington such services, as intitle the latter to the stile and title of an ingrate, and from me that of an inhuman varlet.

Wanted, one or two Journeymen Goldsmiths, and one Journeyman Jeweller, who will meet with good encouragement, as I intend to carry on the business as usual, of which our friends are requested to take notice. Such of Mr. Buell's creditors as he owes small sums to, and dare not stay till I get cash, may immediately be paid in work.

ALETTA BUELL

New-haven, Feb. 21, 1775.

By this time it has become clear to the reader, who I hope is a gentle reader, full of charity for sins of omission, that there are many things about Buell as to which his biographer is ignorant. Here are two or three more to add to a score which I hope no one will tot up. How had Buell become indebted to Rivington to such an extent that the New York printer could secure an attachment against his house and its contents? Hardly in the capacity of silversmith or jeweller could this have occurred; nor is it much more likely that it could have been brought about through experiments in type founding, for there is no evidence that Buell attempted to cast type during the decade 1770 to 1780. There remains then the greater probability that the indebtedness had occurred as the result of transactions in the engraving business which Buell may have carried on more extensively at this time than we realize. In the later section, "The First Connecticut Engraver," this suggestion will be discussed and supported by evidence which is interesting even though not entirely conclusive. But whatever its cause, there is no doubt as to the bitterness of the dispute. If Buell had not been far away at the time, as will soon be demonstrated, he would have experienced understandable satisfaction in attaching himself to that band of Connecticut "Sons of Liberty" who in April, 1775, invaded New York and there attacked and virtually ruined the establishment of the loyalist printer. In this same month and year Rivington had been hanged in effigy in New Brunswick, New Jersey. As patriot and as private enemy of the despised loyalist, Buell would have approved the broadside satirical verses, attributed to Philip Freneau, in which sentiments very uncomplimentary to the supposed speaker are set forth as *The Last Words, Dying Speech, and Confession of J---s R----g--n, P---t-r . . . who was executed at New Brunswick . . . on the Thirteenth Day of April, 1775 . . .*[15] It would give a better balance to the story, of course, if we possessed materials which would enable us to oppose a sketch of Abel Buell by Rivington to the castigation of Rivington by the devoted Aletta. Buell, we have seen, was a man of uncertain temperament and erratic action, while Rivington, perhaps, was not quite the figure of evil he has been painted by Aletta and others of his contemporaries. He was a man of many excellencies and many complexities whose life in New York in the period of the Revolution has found sympathy if not condonation among tolerant historians and biographical writers of today.

FLIGHT TO FLORIDA

A document of the year 1782 verifies the tradition, recorded by John Warner Barber and others, that in this moment of desperation caused by Rivington's action against him for debt, and, as will be seen, by his indebtedness to the State, Buell took himself as far away from Connecticut as could well be done. The ingenious measure of the royal government intended to satisfy claims for services in the French and Indian War, and at the same time provide for the peopling and development of the huge Florida cession of 1763, accounts for the choice of West Florida as the place of refuge to which he now made his way. In 1773 and 1774 a considerable number of Connecticut folk went trustingly southward to take up the lands they expected to find awaiting them.[16] Abel Buell was one of those who joined in this migration. Many years later, on October 16, 1782, Samuel Shethar, "late of Pensacola in the Province of West Florida now residing at Litchfield in the County of Litchfield" petitioned the Connecticut Assembly to declare unlawful the seizure of his goods made while he was in passage from New York to Killingworth in a sloop protected by a flag of truce. We may not continue with Shethar's uncommonly interesting story beyond saying that somewhat later his petition was favorably acted upon by the Assembly. His long memorial is of concern in the present association, however, because of its opening sentences, which read:[17]

"That in the Month of December A D 1774 your memorialist then being an Apprentice to Abel Buell of New Haven in New Haven County went with said Buell in his service to said Pensacola where he continued in the Service of s^d^ Buell till his Apprenticeship expired which was in the Month of April A D 1776. The Communication between the s^d^ Pensacola and the American States being by that Time wholly cut off your Mem^st^. to procure a subsistence entered into Business as a Goldsmith and in the year 1777 there married, and soon after having manifested too openly his Attachment to the Welfare of his native County [*sic*], & his good Wishes for the success of its Arms, was by the Government of West-Florida required to take the Oath of Allegiance to the King of Great Britain, and refusing to comply with such Requisition was compelled to find security in the sum of £1000–Sterling . . ."

In these words we find the only documentation of the tradition that under the pressure of prosecution for debt, Buell fled to Florida and lived there for an undetermined period. The date of departure from Connecticut fits nicely enough with what we know of the incident from another source. On February 21, 1775, Aletta Buell declared in her advertisement, already quoted, that at the time he fled New Haven her husband had left orders with her to bring suit against those of his debtors whose accounts remained unsettled six weeks after his departure, a step which she was now determined to take. We may, therefore, think of Buell as having left New Haven late in December, 1774, for his sojourn in Pensacola. The sentences quoted from the Shethar memorial suggest, furthermore, that he carried on in that place the business of the goldsmith. The memorial leaves us completely uncertain, however, as to how long he remained there. It seems clear enough that he was still in residence in that far place when in April, 1776, his apprentice, Samuel Shethar, became free of his apprenticeship and set up in the business of goldsmith on his own account. That date is the last we have for Buell in Florida. The interesting story related by Barber of his involvement with the British governor is undated.[17a] His relationship with the authorities is unknown, however, as are the means he later employed to remove himself from Florida to Connecticut. In a later section we shall examine somewhat critically one of the legends which has come into being as the result of his Florida residence.

ABEL BUELL,
of Killingworth in Connecticut, Jeweller and Lapidary, begs leave to acquaint the Public, and the Printers of the Several Colonies, that he hath diſcovered the art, and hath alreday entred upon the Buſineſs of founding Types, which as Soon as he can furniſh himſelf with Stock, will ſell for the ſame price at which they are purchaſed in LONDON; in which Buſineſs he hopes for the Encouragement of the Printers, and all American Patriots.

"The first proof struck by American types," 1769, from the only known specimen, among the Stiles papers in the Yale University Library.

Type Founder & Inventor

RETURN FROM EXILE

Buell was one of those men who are successful in their wives. During his absence from New Haven, Mrs. Aletta Buell seems to have carried on his business to greater prosperity than it had attained when he was the acting head of the establishment. In August, 1777, she declared her readiness and ability to repay the sum of £100 advanced by the colony when in the year 1769 her husband proposed the establishment of a type foundry within its borders. She claimed to have acquired this money by her industry in the years of his exile, and she repaid it even though it had been received and spent without benefit to her in the period before she became his wife. He was more involved in debt than she had supposed at first and the earning of the money had been difficult. One would say, indeed, that she had bettered her intention of carrying on the business as usual. Her admirable letter to the authorities is given in full in a later chapter.

Not many days after Aletta's offer to repay her husband's debt had been placed before the Assembly, a resolution of that body, dated simply "August 1777," provided for the return of the bond to her in exchange for the sum of £100 lawful money. While awaiting the consummation of this transaction with the State, Aletta continued to care for and advance her husband's interests. A newspaper advertisement of September 2, 1777, reveals her as having for sale copies of one of the engravings Abel had made before his flight from New Haven, and at the same time serves to bring into our story that eccentric Hollander, Bernard Romans—engineer, geographer, cartographer, writer, publisher, and figure of controversy whose connection with the Buells will be discussed more fully later. At the conclusion of his long advertisement in the *Connecticut Journal* of the day named, Romans made a small gesture of friendship to the wife of a man with whom, I believe, he had been associated some years earlier. The concluding words of the advertisement carry us back to the Yale diplomas that Buell had made at some undetermined time before his exile. The paragraph reads:

> Such Gentlemen as are ready to take their Degrees, may be supplied with blank Diplomas, neatly printed on the very best of Imperial paper, by enquiring of Mrs. Buell.

We applaud this loyal wife and competent woman. We know little of her but all that little is good. The result of her proposal to refund to the State the £100 advanced to her husband to promote the establishment of a type foundry enables us to conclude happily this passage in Buell's story of frustration. On October 17, 1777, the Treasurer of the State entered in his books the payment of £100 from Abel Buell and his surety, Ebenezer Chittenden, and thus, so far as the State was concerned, made possible the return of Buell to Connecticut.[18]

The payment of her husband's debt brings Aletta Buell into our story for the last time. It is probable that she died very soon after this final appearance, having played a role common in that day when wives seemed habitually able to carry on the business of absent or deceased husbands.

MAN OF AFFAIRS

Buell seems to have returned to New Haven soon after the payment of his debt to the State. A question that causes perplexity to one who attempts the relation of his career is that of his whereabouts from the time we last hear of him in Florida in April, 1776, until his reappearance in New Haven some two years later. We place him certainly in Connecticut in May, 1778, with a probability that he was there in October, 1777, when his bond for £100 was repaid the State. Sometime, therefore, between that October date and May, 1778, he returned to Connecticut and prepared for activities more varied and larger in scale than any he had previously attempted. It may be that he had remained in Florida throughout this period or that he was making his way homeward by easy stages. An anecdote which places him in New York in June, 1776, rests upon no evidential basis.[19] We shall have to leave the problem unsolved, assuming that he returned to Connecticut early in 1778 after three years of exile spent chiefly in Pensacola, engaged in the activities of his silversmith's craft or in other tasks which required imagination, skillful hands, and the gift of knowing how to do everything except become a solid, prosperous, and conventional citizen.

By what means Buell's private debts were compounded does not appear. We have seen that his debt to the State was settled in October, 1777, and though the claim against him urged by Rivington was not finally settled until December, 1779, it is probable that at the time of his return to New Haven the "inhuman varlet" who was persecuting him stood little chance as a New York loyalist of pressing successfully a claim in the Connecticut courts.[20] It is likely that with these major claims discharged or, by reason of the political situation, no longer to be feared, an agreement was easily concluded with lesser creditors which permitted his return to New Haven. This we can understand, but once more we are to be faced with the familiar but incongruous situation of the bankrupt, discharged of his obligations, who presents a semblance of prosperity greater than before his fall. On May 19, 1778, Governor Trumbull commissioned as a privateer the sloop *Porcupine*. The vessel was armed with two guns and four swivels and manned by Captain William Stewart and eighteen men. The owners, and here is the cause of our bewilderment, were Abel Buell & Company of New Haven.[21] Even if he could not keep his hold on money and property Buell seems to have possessed the quality of drawing them into his hands. A few months later the *Connecticut Journal* of September 2, 1778, informs us that thereafter at stated times vendues will be held under his management at the Sign of the Coffee Pot, near the State House in New Haven. So recently a wanderer, the bankrupt Buell was soon to become one of the most active men of business in the Connecticut town. Despite his life of continuous experiment in an extraordinary variety of commercial, mechanical, and artistic fields, the vendue he conducted seems to have been for some fifteen years an important consideration in his life, or rather, in his economy. Probably it provided the enduring basis of his livelihood. Advertisements showing the scope and extent of his auctions are found in the *Connecticut Journal* in November, 1778, March, 1779, April and May, 1783, and November, 1791. Doubtless there were others. The 1783 advertisements show him conducting business under the firm name, Buell & Mix. We assume that his partner was the John Mix with whom not long before he had been associated in a second venture in privateering. In what may have been their first announcement, April 2, 1783, the partners assure those who read that "The Purchasers may depend there will be no collusive sales."

From the time of Buell's reinstatement in New Haven in 1778 until the end of the century his life seems to have gone on rather more smoothly than in its earlier period. Soon after his return he was married for the third time. When and how he had lost the faithful Aletta does not appear in the local records, nor does there seem to have been preserved the date of his presumptive marriage to Rebecca (Parkman) Townsend, a woman of a locally prominent family.[22] At any rate this third marriage lasted longer than any of the others and was more productive in children who lived beyond infancy. We may assume that it was a happier, or at least a quieter, union in so far as marital unions are affected by disturbances from without.

The newspaper advertisements of a great part of this time show Abel Buell to have been an active man of affairs, a promoter of enterprises of usefulness to his community, but not always, it is to be feared, of profit to himself. He advertised for sale literally everything from ships to sealing wax; he was auctioneer, proprietor of a line of packet boats that plied between New Haven and New London; he was interested in the development of near-by marble quarries, and during the Revolutionary days, when new printing materials could not be imported, he brought his long-deferred type foundry project to the point where he was able to supply several Connecticut printers with type for their cases.

It seems, moreover, that not even these varied pursuits were enough to occupy Buell's energies, for toward the close of the war he is found engaged once more in the romantic business of privateering. The sloop *Tiger,* carrying two guns and thirty-six men, was commissioned on June 1, 1782. The venture was bonded for $20,000 by the ship's captain, Daniel Jones, with whom were associated Abel Buell, Phineas Bradley, John Mix, Jr., and Samuel Bird, Jr., all of New Haven.[23] The owners in this case were named as Phineas Bradley & Company, and at least one profitable prize fell to the lot of the *Tiger* before the Peace of 1783 put an end to her forays against the enemy's commerce. This event had no sooner occurred, however, than Buell found in it the incentive for a venture of another sort. Treaties and the new political divisions they establish demand new maps, and hardly had the Peace become a fact when Buell set about engraving the large map of the United States that remains as a record of his talent and of his artistic ambitions. The quality of timeliness was a feature of Abel Buell's ventures which invariably forces itself to be noticed, even though in his case timeliness seems seldom to have meant financial profit. The map was published in March, 1784, and five months later its engraver is found putting a mortgage on the lot facing the Green on which stood his shop and dwelling house.[24] The time and material and the publication costs that went into the production of this great map of 41 x 46 inches may well provide a connection of cause and effect between these two apparently unrelated incidents.[25]

MINT MASTER AND MANUFACTURER

Buell's last employment of consequence in the field of engraving was not as print maker but as practitioner of the more ancient craft of sinking or cutting dies for the making of coins. It has just been suggested that the mortgaging of his house in the summer of 1784 had been a means of procuring cash to clear up the publication expenses of his *Map of the United States,* issued in March of that year. It may be, however, that it was not the past which was concerning him at this time. The map was behind him, an old story. A new project was already engaging his attention. I am inclined to believe that he was the initiator of the project, and that its early, experimental stages required from him the outlay of hard money.

The enterprise which now engaged Buell's attention took form in due time as the Company for Coining Coppers.[26] The story of that concern is of interest to the numismatist and the economic historian. It has specific importance, of course, in our consideration of Abel Buell as mechanic and engraver. It has been competently told in outline more than once, and its many complexities have been implied in these relations. Here we must view it strictly in the perspective established by the numerous different activities in which Buell engaged throughout his life.

In its session of October, 1785, the Connecticut Assembly, in response to a memorial dated the 18th of that month, authorized Samuel Bishop, James Hilhouse, John Goodrich, and Joseph Hopkins to establish "a Mint for Coining and Manufacturing Coppers." The pennies were to be in weight and design based upon the current British halfpenny. They were intended for the convenience of trade and were not to be regarded as legal tender in the payment of debts. One-twentieth part of the output of the pennies was to be paid into the State treasury every six months. Acting upon this authorization, the grantees on November 12, 1785, joined to themselves four other men, one of them Abel Buell, and established the Company for Coining Coppers with each proprietor the owner of a one-eighth share in the business. It has never been questioned that it was Buell's skill as mechanic and engraver that formed the core of the enterprise soon to be put into active operation in a building on Water Street in New Haven.

At its January session, 1789, the Assembly appointed a committee to inquire into the manner in which the affairs of the Company were being conducted. Under date of April 9, 1789, this committee submitted a report which was in effect a concise history of the Company up to that day, recording its many changes of stock ownership, its stoppages of work and the conditions under which activities had been resumed. From its beginning until the cessation of operation under the original State authorization, in June, 1787, the Company had submitted for inspection 28,944 pounds of coined coppers, amounting in value to £3908:6:8. The State had received all of its one-twentieth share of the output except the small sum of £8:3. Throughout the period almost the only stockholder whose share had remained constant was Abel Buell. It may be that his share in the Company had been awarded him not through purchase but in recognition of his ownership of the stamping machine and the dies which it employed plus the donation of his services as technical superintendent of the operation. That certainly is frequently the basis upon which an inventor becomes one of the company formed to exploit his ideas. This suggestion of ownership is supported by the closing words of the report in which the Assembly committee said "that Abel Bewel has gone to Europe that previous to his Departure he gave his son Benjamin Bewel Liberty to Coin Coppers which Bussiness he is now persuing and has just begun to Stamp them."

There was no suggestion of improper conduct of the mint in the committee's report, but though both houses accepted it one feels that the members quietly concluded the private minting of pennies had gone on long enough. They brought Benjamin Buell's activities to a close with their order that after June 20, 1789, the mint should cease operations and that all concerned with the Company should appear before the Assembly of the coming October and show reason why their privilege should not be rescinded.

The final closing down of the mint was probably much less a matter of concern to Abel Buell than it would have been if he had not already acquired a new interest. Sometime before April 9, 1789, he had gone to England as a mint master seeking, tradition says, a dependable copper supply. A few years later he returned as a cotton manufacturer with a new dream of success leading him to the establishment of a larger enterprise.

The failure of the coinage scheme as just remarked, did not deter Buell from making another attempt in the grand manner of the promoters of industry. In the year 1789 he raised £150 by a mortgage on his shop,[27] and went to England for the purpose, it was said, of securing copper in quantity for the mint. The fact that when he left New Haven the coinage project was still on his mind gives a basis for the acceptance of this proffered reason for his journey. But whether or not copper was the immediate object of his quest it seems to be true that he soon lost sight of that purpose and returned to America full of a new enthusiasm and agog with practical ideas for its translation into action. The scheme that now engaged him was the construction of a cotton manufactory. It is said that during his stay in England, he worked for a few months in one of the great textile mills and came away with an expert's knowledge of machinery and processes. The length of his apprenticeship in the English mills is nowhere recorded, nor are his immediately subsequent actions known. It is probable that he did not return at once to his New Haven residence, for in a mortgage transfer of March 30, 1793, he is described as "Abel Buell late of New Haven now residing at the cotton manufactory near New York, N.Y."[28] From this suggestive reference we must suppose either that he was continuing his education in the new industry at a New York mill, or that he was aiding in some capacity in the establishment of the business in the metropolis. The industry of cotton weaving was beginning to stir the American imagination, and in Connecticut two coincidental attempts at founding the manufactory are to be observed at this time. We find that the references to these efforts in the *Diary of Ezra Stiles* are of particular interest to us inasmuch as one of the projects discussed by the learned amateur of industries was the mill established by Abel Buell at Westville, New Haven.

On April 15, 1795, Dr. Stiles recorded in his diary the following sentences:[29]

> I rode out with Professor Meigs to view Mr. Buell's Cotton Manufact^{y} 2 M. off. It cost 2000 Dollars, built this year. This is the 2^{d} Manuf^{y} built in this T^{o} within 2 y. Mr. McIntosh's at Bradley T^{o} 2 M. NW fr. T^{o} was built 1794. Cost £10,000. This last is very grand—but will fail, & Buell's will succede, tho' much smaller. . . .

Once more we have encountered Buell in the capacity of industrial pioneer, but the meeting with him this time is very short in duration. We hear no more of that cotton mill, successfully begun, in the story of his career. If we may accept Dr. Stiles's description of it as the second local mill and the first with a successful future before it, its place in the history of the Connecticut mill industry becomes sufficiently clear. One pauses just a moment to admire the sardonic humor of life—to look forward thirty years to Buell's death in a pauper's bed at a time when the bright gold was flowing into the hands of a succeeding generation of mill owners. It was Buell's misfortune that the year of his departure for England and induction into the mysteries of cotton manufacture was also the year of Samuel Slater's departure from England for America, his mind charged with the accumulated knowledge of many years' experience with English spinning machinery and methods. By the time Buell, in 1795, had set up his cotton manufactory in Connecticut, the association of Slater and Moses Brown at Pawtucket, Rhode Island, had radically changed American methods of cotton spinning. Unfortunately we do not know whether Buell's failure to go ahead with his scheme came about because of this competition, through lack of capital, through lack of mastery of his own improved machinery, or through the loss of interest which seems to have prevented others of his plans from coming to the stage of full development.

"AN INGENIOUS MECHANIC"

In the closing years of the century Buell's extraordinary activities in the business world—auctioneer, privateersman, packet boat proprietor, mint master, cotton manufacturer, to name a few of them—seem to have abated. In an advertisement found in several issues of the *Connecticut Journal* following that for May 18, 1796, he has departed the world of commerce and turned back for the means of living to the practice of the several handicrafts in which he excelled. The list of fascinating services he offered his community in those notices reads as follows:

Mariners' and surveyors' compasses and other instruments cleaned and rectified, engraving, seal and die sinking, seal presses, enameled hair worked mourning rings and lockets, fashionable gold rings, earrings and beads, silver, silver-plated, gilt and polished steel buttons, button and other casting moulds, plating mills, printers blacks, coach and sign painting, gilding and varnishing, patterns and models of any sort of cast work; mills and working models for grinding paints as used in Europe; working models of canal locks, drawings on parchment, paper, silk, etc., by Abel Buel, College Street, New Haven, where there is a decent furnished front chamber to let by the week.

Later in this same year, in three November issues of the *Connecticut Journal,* Buell advertised that he had "on exhibition the wonderful negro who is turning white." The authenticity of this phenomenon was vouched for, it may be observed, by Timothy Dwight, president of Yale College. On April 25, 1798, a news item announced a useful machine of Buell's invention for planting onions and corn.

If anything is perceived clearly in the life of Abel Buell it is his inability to direct his projects to a substantial and lasting financial benefit. In 1795 we see him through Dr. Stiles's benevolent spectacles as a mill operator walking a cleared path to success. In 1796 we find the long advertisement from him, just quoted in full, in which he claims the ability to make or to supply almost everything that one might need except the product of a cotton mill. In 1797 he fashions four communion cups for the North Haven Congregational Church. In 1798 he is selling his newly invented corn planter and exhibiting to the curious a negro undergoing the process of albication. A year later his world seems to have fallen to pieces again, and for the second time he turns his back on New Haven. Whether it was the decay of his business in that city which led him to leave it when he was considerably past his middle age, or whether for a moment the city of Hartford held out some particularly rich promise that his eager hopefulness could not resist, we have difficulty in determining. Anyhow in the spring of 1799 we find him removed from New Haven and keeping shop opposite the North Meeting House in Hartford.

It was just at this time that the undeclared French War was agitating the country, and from the character of his Hartford advertisements in the year 1799, we perceive that Buell was riding the wave of popular interest. He has added another ancient craft to his list of accomplishments and become an armorer. In the *Connecticut Courant* for April 22, 1799, and for two succeeding issues he announces "A few good Horsemen's Swords, Army and Navy Officers do. and Hangers, for sale by Abel Buel, Opposite the North Meeting House, Hartford. April 20." For three weeks in September of the same year, beginning with September 16, his advertisements in this paper strike again the military note when he offers "Very Cheap. Silver and silverplated, gilt and silver washed, steel, brass and iron hilted Swords and Dirks: brass and steel Pikes: and Military Flags elegantly painted and gilt, . . . Sept. 16." A year and a half later his activities have broadened: on April 20, 1801, and for the two following issues, he addresses the public in these words:

The subscriber informs the gentlemen of this city and the adjacent country, that he has a good apparatus for repairing, cleaning, and polishing their Military arms of every description, and will thank them for their custom this season. He makes the most approved and fashionable ornaments for military Caps and Cartridge Boxes, paints and gilds Flags, engraves Seals, Dies, Punches, and Copper Plates, marks silver Plate and Rings with elegant Cyphers and Arms; cuts Blocks and Ornaments for

Printers; makes and repairs any common or difficult work, fabricated from metal or wood. The smallest favors will be gratefully acknowledged by their humble servant,

ABEL BUEL

Hartford, April 17, 1801.
Mr. Buel wants two or three young Lads of ingenuity.

We learn from this advertisement that in addition to the making, or perhaps merely the selling, of weapons of the cut and thrust variety, Buell has gone back to the diverse activities of his New Haven days. It is interesting to know that he still "engraves Seals, Dies, Punches, and Copper Plates" and it is a matter that stirs the curiosity of the bookman to learn that he "cuts Blocks and Ornaments for Printers." It would be pleasant to search these out in some time of leisure; certainly if we may judge by the cut which appears at the head of this very advertisement (see illustration facing page 72), such an investigation would be worth the pains. And how happy would our communities be today if they had in them men, or even one man, who "makes and repairs any common or difficult work, fabricated from metal or wood"!

THE CLOSING YEARS

It is not known how Buell's affairs in Hartford progressed. References to his life there are few. On August 19, 1803, he conveyed to Abel Buell, Jr., mariner, of New York, and to Margaret his wife, his lot in the new burial ground of New Haven.[30] Perhaps he soon regretted the transfer of this particular piece of property, for the Hartford Sexton's List shows that ten days later, on August 29, there was buried the "Wife of Abel Buell aged 34 years," and the *Connecticut Courant* for August 31 records the death earlier in the week of "Mrs. Sally Buell, wife of Mr. Abel Buell." In a note (no. 22) on the general subject of Buell's matrimonial ventures the possibility has been mentioned and argued against that the four ladies we have met as Mrs. Abel Buell were the wives of two or more men of the same name. Here I repeat that I have found nothing to lead me to believe that this was the case. There is no conflict of dates to be reconciled and no element of inherent improbability to be explained away. I like to think of Abel Buell as one of those patriarchs of old to whom four wives were but so many incidents in a life crowded with dreams and projects and labor.

Not long after the death of Mrs. Sally Buell, Abel turned his eyes toward a new city of refuge. It is said that he next set up his establishment in the town of Stockbridge, Massachusetts, and it seems that now, in his age, he returned to the employment of his youth and occupied himself in this place as a silversmith. The period of his residence there seems uncertain. In the [Stockbridge] *Farmer's Herald* for March 31, 1810, a stray hog is advertised and its owner requested to inquire for it "of Abel Buel, near Mr. Cyrus Williams' store." That he was living in the same town in 1813 is learned from the local church records. In *Stockbridge, Past and Present,* Miss E. F. Jones preserves a memory of him that is not recorded elsewhere. It shows him to us, as we have seen him to be in all the relations of life, an eccentric, zealous man, putting his whole being into the emotion of the moment. The narrator informs us that Buell had become an infidel through intimate association in England with Tom Paine, but that the religious revival of 1813, when he was still a resident of Stockbridge, had induced in him a change of heart. He became a great reader of the Bible, and finally one day exclaimed to Mr. Swift, a visiting pastor, "They have been altering the Bible! This is not the same book which Tom Paine and I used to ridicule! They have altered it; they have *altered* the Bible. *This* is beautiful! Oh, how beautiful! All beautiful! beautiful, beautiful." Soon afterwards, at more than seventy years of age, he joined the church and remained within the Christian communion until the end. The anecdote seems to find a certain support in the presence of Buell's name in the list of persons who united with the Congregational Church of Stockbridge in the wonderful year of 1813.[31]

Between this time and the end of his life the record is blank. The disabilities of old age forced him to give up his establishment in Stockbridge, and return to New Haven to a death in circumstances dreaded by all mankind. The *Columbian Register* in its issue of Saturday, March 23, 1822, contained the following notice in the obituary column:

> At the Alms House in this town, on the 10th, Mr. Abel Buel, aged 81 years, an ingenious mechanic, . . .[32]

There is no need for comment nor, at this place, for a summary of Abel Buell's services to his community. In the following chapters, the three principal activities of his career will be discussed separately in greater detail than has been done in the foregoing outline of his life.

Jeweller & Silversmith

THE lapidary instrument that Buell invented and offered to the Colony as ransom for his body is said to have been the earliest mechanism of the sort to be constructed in this country. No description remains of its principles, so that we may not know in what essentials it differed from the machines used for cutting and polishing stones in European workshops of the period. Beyond what has already been related concerning it, I have been able to discover few other references to its existence. One of these makes it known that Buell accompanied his last petition to the Assembly by an exhibit in the form of a ring set with semi-precious stones of his own cutting. This article of adornment was sent by its maker to Matthew Griswold, whose influence as attorney-general of the colony naturally would weigh heavily in the outcome of his plea.[33] Its beauty of workmanship, the story goes, was one of the factors that brought about the beneficent action of the Assembly. True or not, we have in this story a genuine Arabian Nights incident engrafted upon our sober New England annals. Change New London to Bagdad and attorney-general to wazir and we should have romance creeping into our matter-of-fact narrative.

A second reference to Buell as lapidary has a document behind it. A few months after the young offender's restoration to liberty, the Reverend John Devotion of Saybrook wrote to the Reverend Ezra Stiles of Newport on the subject of recent industrial developments, then becoming a matter of political as well as of economic interest. The Say-

One of four identical communion cups made by Abel Buell in 1797 for the North Haven Congregational Church. Reproduced through the courtesy of its present owner, Mr. Philip Hammerslough, of West Hartford, Connecticut.

Salt spoons, with "AB" mark, presumably made by Buell, from the collection of the Connecticut Historical Society.

Connecticut pennies, 1785, obverse and reverse. The dies for these were cut by Buell, and the pennies presumably minted by him. Courtesy Connecticut Historical Society.

brook minister assured his correspondent that in this matter of cutting amethysts and other native stones our Killingworth lapidary's "Invention equals his curious neat workmanship."[34] Whether the word "invention" as used here refers to the mechanism itself or to Buell's intelligent artistry may be open to doubt, but it is clear that his employment of the machine in the months following its construction was of such a nature as to win the encomiums of a man of judgment.

A most explicit statement relating to the too brief story of Buell's lapidary machine is found in an advertisement in the *Boston Gazette* for December 7, 1767, communicated to me by Mr. Clarence S. Brigham, in which Buell, opportunistic as always, seeks to tie up his own invention and its use with the popular movement for the encouragement of American manufactures. This announcement of skills and abilities, as has been said in the preceding section, suggests that Buell had taken to the road in the prosecution of his trade as a jeweller. The advertisement is given in full:

Abel Buel
of the Colony of Connecticut
Jeweller and Lapidar,

Begs Leave to acquaint the Gentlemen and Ladies of the Town of Boston, That as the Inhabitants of this Town have generously Resolv'd to encourage the manufactures of the Colonies—These may acquaint them that he hath discover'd the true method of grinding and polishing chrystals and other stones of value, viz. Rubies, Garnets, Topaz, Amethysts, white and brown Chrystals, &c. (with which the American Colonies abound) and that he has [specimens?] of the above kind of stone in the native State; as also ground, polish'd and set; by which any Person may be convinc'd of his knowledge of both Branches of that Business, which he will shew to any Person on change every day of this present Week; and will wait on any Gentlemen or Ladies at their Houses, who are desirous to encourage our own Manufactures (on their sending a Line to him at Mrs. Brackets in Schoolhouse Lane) and will supply them with any Jewellry Ware of the above kind done in the neatest manner from native stones of the Colonies.

A. BUEL.

Here was the "further Enlargement" for which two years earlier Buell had petitioned the Assembly and which, in October, 1766, had been granted him upon his representation that he had perfected a machine for polishing crystals and precious stones.

If we keep in mind the Buell advertisement of May 18, 1796, reproduced in the preceding section, we must assume that Buell employed himself to the same extent as other active and busy men of his trade in fashioning articles of personal adornment and utility. There must have been ready sale in his community for those watch cases, fobs, shoe buckles, and brooches upon which some of the most charming craftsmanship of the period was expended. Peculiarly liable to loss and to the mischances of "wear and tear," relatively few of them survive; sold without the maker's mark, the attribution of extant specimens to the hand that fashioned them is a matter of the greatest difficulty. In the normal course, he would have made and sold many such trinkets and articles of usefulness.

THE JEWELLER'S STOCK IN TRADE

Before we leave Buell the Jeweller to speak of Buell the Silversmith, we must examine an inventory of his New Haven shop which makes explicit the generalizations just expressed. To do this we return to that unhappy day in February, 1775, when a constable, with the writ granted James Rivington in his hand, listed the articles of household utility and the jewelry stock he had attached in obedience to its terms. It is interesting to learn from this list the number and nature of the articles which a modest jewelry shop in New Haven kept in stock in February, 1775.[35] ". . . I attached," says the constable, [*separating commas supplied by the author*] "three Desks, one square Table, 5 red [reed?] Bottom York Chairs, 1 Great Chair do, 1 Large Gilt Looking Glass, 1 writing Desk, one Plated Coffee pot, 2 plated butter boats, one Silver hilted Sword, 3 pinch back Cane heads, 8 Japan Sugar Tongs, 6 Snuff Boxes, 16 Silver Thimbles, 1 Case of Tooth Instruments, 5 Silver plated Spurs, 14 pr black Jet Sleeve buttons, 4 pearl Necklaces, 9 black Do., 2 pinch back broches, 3 white mettle Do., 1 Silver Do., 1 Cucumber plane, 1 pinch back Needle Case, 1 Japan Sugar Tonges, 3 Drill Bows, 2 Slate Bookes, 19 hanks Skillet wire, 1 pinch Back Broch, 4 Do., 6 pr blk Jet Buttons, 3 Silver Decanter Labels, 10 pinch back Stock buckels, 1 Do., 10 Steel watch Chains, 37 Watch Keys, 9 pinch back watch Seals, 1 Silver Do., 1 Common Do., 4 Brass Escutcheons, 2 Fountain pens, 2 Steel watch Seals, 2 Stay Hooks, 11 pr Pibble Sleeve Buttons, 5 pr Silver Stone Buttons, 5 Do. Silver Stone Jewels, 8 pr pinch back Sleve Buttons, 1 pinch back ring, 3 pinch back hair Locketts, 2 Silver Do., 42 pr pinch back shoe Buckels, 9 pr plated do., 3 pr Steel Do., 5 pr Plated knee Do., 3 pr Gilt Shoe Buckels, 406 Files, one Gross cyphre [2 *words illegible*], 8 Doz. Brilliant paste Ear ring Drops [?], 6 Gross Buckel Stones . . ."

It is difficult to know how many, if any, of these articles were of Buell's making. Many of them, probably, were manufactured articles of import of the cheaper variety obviously not intended for the carriage trade. One would like to know more about the fountain pens of that era, why "Tooth Instruments" were sold by the jeweller, what was the employment of "Skillet Wire," what were "Pibble Sleeve Buttons," and what was the need for a stock of "406 Files." In general, however, the articles of the list are familiar and such as can readily be visualized in use upon the persons of the New Haven neighbors, some of them perhaps, adorning the students of Yale College, to whom the engraver of the College diploma, Buell, would certainly have been known. One article found in the list continues to tease the imagination. What was a "Cucumber plane?" Many persons, at my solicitation, have offered interpretations of the name, nature, and use of the implement thus designated. The most likely suggestion has been made by a thoughtful carpenter[35a] who brought to me what he called a "cooper's plane," an antique, or relatively antique, tool acquired by him a good many years ago in Vermont. The oak stock of the plane is fashioned in the shape of an arc of about one-fourth of a circle. The blade emerges from the stock well forward of its center. The special use of the plane was to smooth the top edges of the staves of a newly hooped barrel. The plane was pushed around the circle formed by the protruding ends of the staves, held in position by a wooden flange, attached to the inner side of the stock and cut to the same curvature, which fitted snugly the inner circumference of the circle. The plane now in my hands shows a deep groove worn in its base, or sole, forward of the blade, an indication of long service in its special employment. Planes of this sort would have been of different degrees of curvature according to the circumference of the barrels or casks upon which they were to be used. Measurements and calculations make clear that the specimen before me was intended for use upon barrels of about nineteen inches diameter at the head. It is not at all unlikely that one of lesser curvature intended for use upon a larger cask or a hogshead could have been called in New Haven or elsewhere in 1774 a "cucumber plane" because of its chance resemblance to the familiar garden fruit. By transference the term would be applied to all planes of the same general shape and employment. This is as far as I have been able to go in explanation of the country term found in the list of Buell's confiscated possessions.

THE SILVERSMITH

From various advertisements in the *Connecticut Journal* it is known that Buell maintained for many years in New Haven his establishment with the address, much favored by silversmiths of the period, "At the Sign of the Coffee Pot." In 1775, when the circumstances previously related had driven him from the city, his wife advertised for "one or two Journeymen Goldsmiths, and one Journeyman Jeweller," and added the reassuring clause, "as I intend to carry on the business as usual." It is true also that Buell continued the practice of his silversmith's craft intermittently throughout the whole of his life, but on his return to New Haven in 1777 he seems almost at once to have enlarged the range of his activities by engaging in the curiously varied enterprises that have been described. It is likely that from this time the exercise of his fundamental craft suffered neglect in favor of more exciting ventures. Even if allowance be made for this relegation of his earliest interest to a subordinate place in his thoughts as well as for the many interruptions to his business from within and without, one would still expect to find in existence a number of examples of the art that could be attributed to his hand. In his work, *Early Silver of Connecticut,* Mr. George Munson Curtis wrote that in addition to the four communion cups in his collection a number of other pieces made by Buell were extant. He did not specify the nature or whereabouts of these pieces, and, with one probable exception, those of recent years who have sought and listed Connecticut silver have failed to find any of them. The exception is the pair of salt spoons showing the maker's mark, A B, found today in the collections of the Connecticut Historical Society. These are unhesitatingly attributed to Buell by Mr. Philip Hammerslough, learned collector of Connecticut silver and present owner of two of the four communion cups (described and illustrated by Mr. Curtis) which Buell made in 1797 for the North Haven Congregational Church.[36] One of these cups is illustrated, facing page 32, through the courtesy of Mr. Hammerslough.

So expressive are these austerely conceived cups of the excellent workmanship of the period that after seeing them one regrets all the more the failure to identify other examples of Abel Buell's taste and skill in the art of silversmithing.

One incident recorded in connection with Buell's activity as a silversmith partakes of that quality of frustration which seems to be inseparable from his undertakings. Soon after October, 1771, he was engaged by a committee of the Assembly to make a piece of plate of the value of £150 sterling to be presented by the colony to its London agent, Richard Jackson, then a popular official. In the May session of 1773, the committee reported that thirty-eight pounds and some shillings had been advanced to Buell to procure materials for the piece, that the time for the presentation was drawing near, that the piece had not been completed and that Buell could neither finish the work in time nor refund the money. The commission was thereupon taken from Buell and placed elsewhere, and this chance for acquiring distinction in his craft was accordingly lost to him.[37]

In seeking for an explanation of Buell's apparent lack of industry in the exercise of the craft in which he had been trained, it is easy to overlook a factor which may explain the anomaly. From what we know of him, it is clear that he was afflicted with instability of temperament. He had the inventor's spiritual need for new forms of expression, and his attention was continually being diverted from the process of breadwinning by the delightful suggestions of wealth and fame to be obtained through the devices that his imagination taught him to build. To carry through ideas with sober, day-by-day industry was a chore for lesser men, the useful but not important men who act upon ideas but do not conceive them. Why should a man of universal genius stick to the routine of the silversmith's craft when just beyond the workshop door Fame stood beckoning in the guise of engraving, type founding, lapidary machines, machines for minting coins, map making, and new processes for the spinning and weaving of cotton?

Type Founder

THERE is to be observed a parallelism between the origin of certain of the crafts in colonial America and the early stages of the same crafts in medieval Europe. Line engraving and etching seem to have had their beginnings in the goldsmith's practice of taking rubbings of his incised designs in order to preserve their patterns. The next step in the progress of the art is obvious. Before long there came into being the goldsmith-engraver, and then in the course of things, the specialized engraver or print maker. In many cases this was a goldsmith's apprentice whose first use of the graver had been on a dish, a sword hilt, a piece of hollow ware, or a belt plate.

In America a similar concurrence in occupations is to be observed. Paul Revere silver and Paul Revere prints are equally in demand by the collector of antiquities. Amos Doolittle of New Haven was coincidentally silversmith and engraver. Examples of the skill in metal work of Thomas Sparrow, the Maryland silversmith, are less easily found than his poorly executed engravings, scarce as copies of these have become. Instances of a similar nature are to be found in the pages of Dunlap and of Stauffer. In the case of Abel Buell, who to his work in the precious metals, to lapidarianism, and to engraving added the art of type founding, an interesting identity of experience and occupation is to be found with the very protagonists of the printing trade, Gutenberg and Fust. The first of these is said to have discovered an improved method of polishing precious stones and is known to have perfected afterwards the cutting and casting of type; Fust was a goldsmith whose encouragement and practice of the new art of casting type provided the impetus it needed to become effective in commercial use.

It is well understood that the adoption by the American colonists of that policy of passive resistance which we know as "non-importation" resulted in the establishment of many of the great manufacturing industries of the United States. In the printing trade before the year 1765, the shops had been dependent for their presses, type, and ink almost entirely on importation from or through Great Britain. Paper alone of their necessities before this time had been manufactured in quantity by American mills, but during the ten-year period from 1765 to 1775, there occurred in different parts of the country the origin of press building as a commercial enterprise, the regular, rather than the occasional, manufacture of printing ink, and the establishment of at least two foundries for the making of printing types. In the last named of these activities, Abel Buell is remembered as the first practitioner to attain something like success. The story of his effort appeals to us from several standpoints.

"OUR AMERICAN GENIUS"

At some time in the two or three years of residence in Killingworth following the restoration of his civic rights, Buell began those experiments in the making of type by reason of which he has attained a place in the typographical annals of his country. The earliest reference to his successful acquirement of this craft is found in a letter which Ezra Stiles, then of Newport, received from a correspondent in Saybrook. "Our American Genius, Abel Buell," so wrote Mr. John Devotion, "is now manufacturing Tipes for printing. Dr. Gale thinks they will be equal to any European ones; the Dr. designs a present of enough of them to print an Advertisement, to your American Society."[38] This foreshadowing of the rise of an important industry took on a more definite shape a day or two later when Ezra Stiles received a communication from Dr. Benjamin Gale, a Killingworth physician and publicist who seems to have maintained for Buell something more than a neighborly interest. Dr. Gale wrote as follows:[39]

Killingworth 1 Aprill 1769

Rev^d^ & Dear S^r^

I send to your Care, & to afford you some pleasure & Satisfaction, in the prosperity of your Country, some Types made by Buel our Lapidary which are ready set for an Advertisement which I request you would take some Care in transmitting seasonably to Dr Chauncy. You will see by reading my Letter to him that the thing must not be known or hinted untill the same Advertisement appears in the Philadelphia Papers & I think for very good Reasons which you will read and consider, and as doubtless you will accompany this with a Letter of your own, I hope you will enforce. I think there are near 40 presses in America, a Sett of Types costs £300 Sterling and they do not last more than 7 or 8 Years; the saving to America will be considerable annually & he tells me he can do the Business to profit. He will want some Stock to set up. I shall strongly recommend it to the Society to do something for him & to encourage the same in other Capital Towns. I propose sending an Advertisement to N York likewise, as I will likewise to you if you request it seasonably. If any thing in that way is done for him it must be done while the thing is fresh & new. Humane Nature is as it is & we must treat it accordingly. If you want to have a Set of Types you must either procure him some old Types—or if you could get a pound or two of Bismuth, I think all the Metals of which Types are composed are to be had in America, unless it be Bismuth, & I very much suspect that is likewise. However as Buel is jealous of his being intercepted by Mein you will not mention Bismuths entring that Composition.

Your most Ob^t^ Hum^b^ Servt

B. Gale

On receiving this letter with the accompanying types, composed for the press, Dr. Stiles bestirred himself in a manner indicative of interest. It was probably in the office of Solomon Southwick, the Newport printer, that the first proofs of Buell's announcement were taken, and it is easy to imagine the printer and his journeymen with their heads together over the little specimen of a manufacture so replete with possibilities of importance to them and to their fellows in American printing-offices. Dr. Stiles sent straightway to Benjamin Gale one of the proofs which Southwick and his men had made, and accompanied it by a letter embodying the criticism the printers had expressed of the new type. So much may be learned from the letter that Dr. Gale sent in reply a few days later. In its lively and vigorous sentences one perceives that it was the political rather than the literary aspect of Buell's achievement which was stirring the imagination of this Killingworth scientist, already known for his enthusiasm in the encouragement of American manufactures. There is a perceptible note of elation in the following communication:[40]

Killingworth 12 Aprill 1769

Rev^{d} & Dear S^{r}

I receiv^{d} y^{r} fav^{r} p^{r} Lewis and note the Contents—Thank you for your care & kindness in procuring me the Slips of Grapes—I have shewn the Proof you sent me to Buel, he will Correct & Amend the Errors of which he is very Capable—any Alterations that may be suggested to him by the printers, he is Able to Execute to their Minds—Will send the Deficient & defective Letters soon, You will retain them in your own Hands till they Arive—as ye other is not yet sent to Philadelphia. I have thought of your retaining these in Your own Hands till the Advertisement is Printed in Philadelphia, then give them one Impression in y^{r} Paper, & Immediately Forward them to Dr Chauncy—I believe it will be well to send the Anecdote relative to Buel's Former Character to Dr Chauncy—These Types are the first Buel ever made & the first Proof struck by American Types.

I make no Doubt but it will highly Alarm the Type founders in Eng[d]. Let them fret in their Grease—they will I trust be more Carefull of Acts of Parliament in Future—this Branch will affect but few & consequently have but Little Operation.

I believe they will soon have enough to do at Home, which will afford them but Little time to plague us—our Efforts for Liberty in America will Exert the same spirit there, which has been long Crampt by Ministerial Influences, standing Armies &c.

I am Dear S[r]
Your Most Ob[t] &
Most Hum[b] Serv[t]
B. GALE

To D[r] Stiles

THE "FIRST PROOF STRUCK BY AMERICAN TYPES"

It may never be known whether Dr. Stiles thought it advisable, in accordance with the suggestion of his correspondent, to secure the publication of Buell's advertisement in the local newspaper, for there are recorded no copies of the *Newport Mercury* for the issue of April 24, 1769, and it does not appear in the issue of April 17, nor in any of the issues of that year which followed the receipt of Dr. Gale's letter. Furthermore there are known to exist none of the separate proofs of the advertisement which were made under the direction of Dr. Stiles in Newport, so that the earliest printed impressions of these types are not available for examination. In this matter, however, we are fortunate. Dr. Stiles sent the stick of type transmitted from Killingworth to his friend, the Reverend Charles Chauncy of Boston, who, in his turn, became interested in the work of the Killingworth craftsman and carried it to the office of Edes & Gill, where, "to gratifie my own curiosity," as he wrote, he ordered three copies of the announcement to be printed. On May 8, 1769, he sent to Dr. Stiles one of the proofs taken for him at this time, accompanied by the letter from which these facts have been learned.[41] With that letter the proof remains today among the Stiles papers in the possession of Yale University, and from this original copy, probably the only one remaining, it is reproduced (facing page 16) through the courteous permission of its present owners. As a display of the first types known to have been cut and cast in English America, this humble advertisement deserves to take rank with other historic specimens of the type founder's art. The words of the announcement, one readily admits after reading them in the facsimile, express an optimism and a spirit of self-congratulation not justified by the crudity of design and execution displayed in the types in which they are set.

"It is very extraordinary," Chauncy commented in his accompanying letter "that such a specimen sh^{d} be made without instruction, from the mer force of Genius; and the man that was capable of this, must be capable of making his letters still more perfect. . . . If Mr. Buell would accomplish this, all who have seen the specimen agree that the letters would be as handsome as those that come from Home."

It is not certain that other specimens of the new letters were sent to Philadelphia and New York for publication in the newspapers. If, because of the imperfections that showed in the proof, Dr. Gale thought better of his earlier intention of widespread newspaper publication, he was not deterred by this consideration from sending samples of the types to the American Philosophical Society of Philadelphia. As both Gale and Stiles were members of this influential society, it was natural that they should turn to it eagerly with their evidence of a possible new industry which would make the country, by that much, less dependent upon England. On May 3, 1769, the "types made by Abel Buel of Connecticut" were referred by the Society to one of its printer members, Thomas Bradford, for examination and report. At the meeting of June 16, 1769, there was read to the Society "Mr. Gale's letter of inquiry about Abel Buel's types," and on June 30 the committee "on Buel's types reported the metal good, & that they doubt not he will correct the defects that appear—different sizes, standing out of line, & the impression of some being too faint." In spite of these faults, the merit of the attempt was recognized by the Society and it was ordered that thanks be conveyed to the founder "for his spirited & useful undertaking" and "that a specimen of Caslon & Son be sent him for his imitation."[42]

The news of Buell's success in making printing types was not long in becoming public knowledge. A few months after the occurrences that have been recorded, on September 4, 1769, the *Massachusetts Gazette* published the following item of news: "We are assured by a Gentleman from the Westward that Mr. Able Buell, of Killingworth in Connecticut, Jeweller and Lapidary, has lately, by his own Genius, made himself Master of the Art of Founding Types for Printing. Printing Types are also made by Mr. Mitchelson of this Town [Boston] equal to any imported from Great-Britain; and might, by proper Encouragement, soon be able to furnish all the Printers in America at the same price they are sold in England." The only other reference I have found by a contemporary to the Mitchelson activities is in the form of a statement by Isaiah Thomas who at the time in question was active in the printing world of Boston. In his *History of Printing in America* (2d ed. 1874, I: 27) Thomas wrote: "An attempt was made to establish a foundry for casting types at Boston about 1768, by a Mr. Mitchelson from Scotland, but he did not succeed."[43]

THE SECOND SPECIMEN AND THE SUBSIDY

Encouraged by the interest of his friends and neighbors, and aided by the criticism of the Newport printers and the American Philosophical Society, "Our American Genius" now determined upon the further promotion of his project. In its October session of the year 1769, the Connecticut Assembly entertained a petition from Abel Buell in which he implored help for the continuance of his venture in type founding on a commercial scale. As a proof of the state of forwardness the new accomplishment had reached in his hands, the petition was presented in the form of a signed broadside printed in types of his own making, showing a letter of a thin face, Long Primer in size, different in design and superior in execution to the letters which composed his earlier specimen. Our facsimile of this "Memorial" (facing page 48), printed originally in red ink, is first to be perused as a text which carries forward our story and then examined as a physical production which makes visually plain the advance in skill Buell had achieved since the printing of his trial specimen six months before. The reproduction has been made from the copy, one of two known, in the Yale University Library, and is shown through the courtesy of the Library authorities.

Upon receiving Buell's "Memorial," interesting to them in both form and contents, the House appointed a committee to examine its pretensions. The actual copy of the "Memorial" presented by Buell to the Assembly is found today in the Connecticut State Library.[44] Attached to it is the report upon its matter submitted by the committee. This document of unusual interest in the history of type founding in the United States reads as follows:[45]

Wee the Subscribers being appointed a Com^tte^ by the Honble House, to take under consideration the Memorial of Abel Buell, Imputing, that he hath discovered the Art of Letter Founding &c—

Begg leave to Report that wee have conferred with s^{d} Buell on the Subject Matter of his Memorial, and are fully convinced that he hath Discovered the Art of Letter Founding; & that he is Capable of makeing Instruments necessary for the proper Apparatus of Letter Founding—and thereupon to Encourage said Buell to prosecute said Business, Recommend it to the Honble House, That there be paid unto s^{d} Buell out of the Publick Treasury the Sum of £100—on his giving his own Bond for £200. Conditioned that provided he pursue makeing the necessary Apparatus for Letter Founding, for the space of one year, next after the receiving s^{d} £100—and doth not depart from this Colony to Inhabit elsewhere, within the space of seven years from the date of said Bond then the Obligation to be void, otherwise to remain in full force.

And in case said Buell pursues the business of makeing Materials for the purpose afores^{d} in a laudable manner for the space of one Year as afores^{d}. That there be then paid out of the Publick Treasury unto s^{d} Buell, one other £100—on his giveing Bond with Surety in the Sum of £200—that he will repay said £100 last mentioned, at the expiration of Seven Years from the date of s^{d} bond, without Interest, & dureing said Term carry on the business of Letter Founding in this Colony—in that case the bond to be null & void, otherwise to remain in full force.

	G. SALTONSTALL	
Octr 21. 1769	N. WHITING	The
	SETH WETMORE	Com.
	THEOP^{s}. MORGAN	

The document containing this report is endorsed by the clerks of both houses of Assembly in the following terms:

This Report is accepted, with alteration, That both ye Sums proposed shall be only lent without Interest & to be repaid at ye end of 7 years from ye Time of receiving, & y^{t} s^{d} Buell find good Security, for such repaym^{t}.

& y^{t} a bill in form may be brot in accordingly.

TO THE HONORABLE THE GENERAL ASSEMBLY OF THE COLONY OF CONNECTICUT, Convened at New-Haven the Second Thurſday of October AD 1769:

The Memorial of ABEL BUELL of Killingworth Humbly ſheweth;

That your Memorialiſt having Experienc'd the Great Goodneſs of this Honorable Aſſembly, for which he Begs Leave to render his moſt Grateful Tribute of thanks, and to Aſſure them from a Grateful Senſe of their Clemency he has made it his unwearied Study to render himſelf Uſeful to the Community in which he lives and the American Colonies in general, and by his Unwearied application for a number of months paſt has Diſcover'd the Art of Letter-Founding: And as a Specimen of his abilities Preſents this Memorial Impreſs'd with the Types of his Own manufacture, and whareas by an Antient Law of this Colony, this Aſſembly were Graciouſly Pleaſed to Enact that any one who ſhould make any Uſeful Diſcoveries ſhould Receive an Encouragment there-for from this Honorable Aſſembly; and as the Manufacture of Types is but in Few hands even in EUROPE, he humbly Conceives it to be a moſt Valuable Addition to the American Manufacture, and as the Expence of erecting a Proper Foundrey will be Great and beyond the abilities of your Memorilaiſt, he humbly hopes for Encouragement from this Aſſembly Either by Granting him the Liberty of a Lottery for Raiſing a Sum Sufficient to enable him to carry on the ſame, or in ſome other way as to this Honorable Aſſembly may ſeem meet; and your Memorialiſt as in duty Bound ſhall ever Pray.

The memorial to the Assembly of October, 1769, printed in the second font of type made by Abel Buell. Reproduced in facsimile from the Yale University Library copy. Another copy is in the Connecticut Archives. The original was printed in red.

In accordance with these terms of acceptance, a resolution, dated simply October, 1769, was drawn, presented, and assented to by the Assembly,[46] and save for the obstruction of human frailty, the way was clear for the development in Connecticut of an industry important to the whole of English America.

The committeemen of the Assembly who recommended state aid to Buell's project seem to have given intelligent consideration to the promotion of the industry which he proposed to establish. When they had satisfied themselves as to the truth of his pretensions, that he was indeed able to cut punches and to make matrices and molds—"the proper Apparatus of Letter Founding," as their report reads—they recommended to the Assembly that he be subsidized to employ himself for the first year in the making of these essential "Materials." After that had been done he might proceed with the process of letter founding. The Assembly resolution, however, makes no distinction in the processes; his grant of aid was given, without qualification, for the establishment of a letter foundry, but it was probably understood between Buell and the committee that his procedure was to be that which they had suggested in their report of October 21, 1769. The wisdom of this provision for a slow and well-founded beginning is clear enough, but in the very perfection of its groundwork may lie the secret of the failure to take form that now occurred in the embryonic type founding industry.

"HUMANE NATURE IS AS IT IS"

The immediate sequence of events is not clearly understood. From a phrase in a letter to the Assembly written by Mrs. Aletta Buell several years later, soon to be quoted, it seems likely that the loan was not advanced until some time after August of the following year. In order to avail himself of the advantages offered to his venture by residence in a larger community, Buell had determined before this time to remove to New Haven, and in this town he was to be found within less than a twelvemonth after the promise of aid had been accorded by the Assembly. There is evidence of a sort that soon after this he made at least the beginnings of an effort to establish his foundry, for we must assume that Dr. Stiles had Buell's work in mind when he wrote in his Diary on May 9, 1775, that "Types were made at N Haven years ago." This entry in the personal diary of one who earlier had been interested in Buell's progress is the only indication yet discovered that he made efforts to carry on his useful craft at any time during the twelve years that followed his acquirement of its processes, and, however earnest these initial efforts may have been, it is certain that they were not successful. He did not make sufficient progress with the establishment of his foundry to justify the authorities in paying him the second sum of £100 authorized by the Assembly in 1769. This loan was to be allowed him only on the condition that he should have pursued the business of making the apparatus of letter casting "in a laudable manner for the space of one year" after the payment of the first subsidy. He may have found the difficulties of quantity production too much for his knowledge of the craft, or, it may be that the necessity for making a living by means of his regular business precluded on his part the assiduity which the secondary craft required of its practitioner. Or, we may look in the same direction for the reason of this defection that our eyes have followed in other instances of failure on Buell's part. "If any thing in that way is done for him it must be done while the thing is fresh & new. Humane Nature is as it is & we must treat it accordingly." So wrote Dr. Gale in his letter of April 1, 1769, concerning Buell and his type founding project. No man is completely a hero to the village doctor.

ALETTA CLEANS UP

Whatever may have been the causes for Buell's failure to prosecute the business of type founding, it is certain that too great a prosperity was not one of them. Affairs went from bad to worse until, by means of a notice in the *Connecticut Journal* of February 22, 1775, signed by Mrs. Aletta Buell, given in full in an earlier section, his world was apprised that because of debt he had been compelled to leave the town. When the Assembly met two years later, in August, 1777, one of the things which came before it for consideration was the petition from Mrs. Buell expressed in the following letter:[47]

SIR

The long absence of my husband makes me almost despair of ever seeing him again & had I not been in continual expectation of that happiness I would ere now have addressed you on the present Subject. When he left me it was unknown to me that he was so much involved as he was, and in a very few days every thing was seized from me, I have by dint of Industry got together so much that I can now refund the money which he had of the State. I always understood that he was to have it during Seven Years without Interest & I believe that period not yet elapsed. If therefore the One hundred pounds can be accepted in full for the dimand against us I am ready to pay it whin ever required, and I hope that the Interest be not expected as I have hard work to do what I now offer, especially as it is money he received before my time & I have never had any [*sic*] enjoyed any benefit from it. Pray write me an anser by next post. I am

Sir Your very hble Servt

ALETTA BUELL

Newhaven August 8, 1777

A few days after Aletta Buell's letter of August 8 had been brought before it, the Assembly granted the request it contained for the clearance of her husband's account with the State. The following resolution is dated "August 1777":[48]

Whereas this Assembly at their Session in October 1769 granted to Abel Buel of Killingsworth the sum of one Hundred Pounds Lawfull money by way of Loan for the Term of Seven years without interest to enable him to set up the business of Letter founding, and the said Buel received said sum of the Treasurer of this State and gave his bond with surety, and Lodged the same with said Treasurer, and whereas the said Buel hath wholly failed to set up & practice said Art, and hath since become insolvent and is abscondide, and Mrs Alletta wife of said Abel having represented to this Assembly that she hath with the utmost difficulty procured the principal sum and praying that the same may be received in full discharge of said bond.

Resolved by this Assembly That Saml Bishop Junr Esqr of New Haven be and he is hereby appointed and authorized and directed to receive of the Treas^r^ the aforesaid bond, and to receive of said Mrs Buell the said sum of one Hundred pounds Lawfull money and give up said bond and deliver the said money to the Treasurer of this State and take his receipt therefore, and Lodge the same with the Secry of this State.

Pass'd in the Lower House
Attest Benj Huntington Clerk
Concurr'd in the upper House
Test George Wyllys Secr'y.

Some weeks passed before the completion of the procedure so carefully laid down in the foregoing resolution of the Assembly. It was not, in fact, until October 17, 1777, that the Treasurer of the State entered on his books the sum of £100 as cash received from "Abel Buell & Ebenezer Chittenden in full of their bond to Gov & Co."[49] The occurrence of Ebenezer Chittenden's name in connection with the redemption of the bond is our first intimation that Buell's former master, brother-in-law, and present neighbor in New Haven had become his surety at the time the money for the type foundry had been advanced. We can imagine the fullness of Ebenezer's admiration for the industrious Aletta Buell, who had made possible his release from the more unpleasant obligation of a bondsman. The completion of the transaction by the Treasurer's entry of October 17th, quoted above, marked the end of the effort made by the Colony eight years earlier to establish in English America the important industry of type founding.

TYPE FOUNDING RESUMED

Unfortunate in many things, Buell seems to have been favored beyond the run of mankind in the number of second chances that destiny held out to him. When in the year 1781, the opportunity occurred for him to resume his efforts at letter casting, it seems that he was able to carry the undertaking to a happier conclusion than that which befell his earlier venture. It is only another evidence of the irony of things that this second and more successful engagement in the operation of a foundry has left behind no documentary records from which its history may be written with enduring satisfaction. A reasonably coherent story, however, may be constructed by bringing certain ascertainable facts to the support of tradition.

It is as one of Buell's numerous concurrent business ventures that we look at the resumption of his type founding project in this period. In the issue of the *Connecticut Journal* for April 19, 1781, a house was announced for sale in a small square of type of an appearance entirely different from the worn and obscure letter in which the remainder of the paper was printed. The new letter was Long Primer in size, and, like the specimen in Buell's memorial of 1769, which it resembled in general appearance, if not in every detail of execution, it showed a thin, wiry face, not perfectly aligned, but possessing the signal advantage to its user of a greater legibility than the battered letters which most of the American newspapers were compelled to print from in the later years of the Revolution. On April 26, a week after the first appearance of this type in the *Connecticut Journal,* an advertisement in that newspaper made known that there were "Wanted Immediately two or three likely young Lads, which the Subscriber will instruct in several ingenious mechanical Arts." The subscriber was Abel Buell, and we may be excused for believing that type founding was one of the mechanical arts in which he needed apprentices when we learn that on May 2, 1781, three columns of the *Journal* were printed in the letter that has been described. The amount of this type used in the paper increased gradually throughout the summer until, on September 6, almost the entire sheet was printed in the letter which we are assuming was from the foundry of Abel Buell.

The publishers of the *Connecticut Journal* were Thomas and Samuel Green, members of a family notable in three successive centuries of American typographical annals. Another member of that family, their brother, Timothy Green, was the proprietor of the *Connecticut Gazette* of New London. Beginning with October 5 of this year, the *Gazette* also appeared in the letter that earlier had supplanted the worn faces of the *Journal.* Timothy Green made further use of this type in his issue of Freebetter's *New England Almanack* for 1783, and it was employed by the printer of Bickerstaff's *Almanack* for 1782,[50] published by N. Patten of Hartford. It was used also in at least one other Patten imprint of the year 1783; that is, in a sermon by Timothy Allen entitled *Salvation for all Men, Put Out of all Dispute.*[51] Doubtless a search would disclose other wartime publications of Connecticut printers in which the distinctive but still improvable letter was made to serve in place of the long worn-out fonts of an earlier importation.

If there exists contemporary evidence proving that the type shown in the *Connecticut Journal* was made by Abel Buell of New Haven, I am forced to confess that it has eluded my search. In lieu of such evidence it is necessary to recapitulate the following facts and circumstances: (a) Buell's ability to manufacture type, (b) the close resemblance of the *Connecticut Journal* type, as it may be called, to the type of the Buell Memorial of 1769, (c) Buell's residence in New Haven during the months that this letter was being supplied little by little to the *Journal,* (d) his advertisement, coincident with the first use of the new letter, for apprentices to be instructed by him in "several . . . mechanical arts." With these facts in mind, one is prepared to accept the tradition preserved by local historians that he engaged energetically in the activity of type founding during this period. One of these writers affirms more specifically that, in a foundry maintained in the old Sandemanian Meeting House in New Haven, Buell employed fifteen or twenty boys in the casting of type.[52]

There remains to be adduced the testimony of Isaiah Thomas, a contemporary living in an adjoining state, himself a printer and a student of the typographical features of the books and newspapers of his day. Always well-informed when it is a question of New England printing history, Thomas says that Buell made several fonts of Long Primer and that "some persons in the trade made use of them."[53] Although he does not specify the date at which this patronage of the foundry occurred, one may accept his statement as corroborative of our belief that the types used in the years 1781 to 1783 by the Greens of New Haven and of New London and by the printer of the works issued by Patten of Hartford were made in a foundry operated by Abel Buell.

As a summary of Buell's contribution to the establishment of type founding in America, it may be said that in the year 1769 he cut and cast two small fonts of type from which were printed proofs existing today in known copies of undoubted authenticity; that because of this achievement he must be regarded in the present state of our knowledge as the earliest of American type founders. He enlarged these fonts by no measurable quantity of type until the year 1781, at which time, there is good reason to suppose, he resumed his efforts and supplied the type which appeared in that year in the newspapers and in other publications of at least two Connecticut printing houses. More than this, however, may not be claimed for him. In the year 1775, during his period of inactivity, the beginning of successful commercial type founding had been instituted by Jacob Bay and Justus Fox, mechanics employed in the establishment of Christopher Sower of Germantown, Pennsylvania.[54] So it happened that the first American practitioner of the art of letter casting failed to convert that art into an industry, an ending familiar to stories of inventive enterprise.

PHILADELPHIA, March 27.

The Commissioners appointed to examine and burn the old Continental money, called in by tax, have proceeded in the business, and according to order of Congress have burnt three millions three hundred and nine dollars and one third of a dollar; and the public are informed, that there are large sums in the several offices ready for the same purpose.

The persons holding bank notes bearing interest, dated on or before the 10th of Sept. 1780, are requested to bring them in for payment, with interest to the 22d inst. And those who have notes, on demand, are desired to apply immediately, for the same purpose, as the accounts

TO BE SOLD,
and entered on immediately,

A Dwelling-House, Barn, and 25 Acres of Land, on Durham Road, about 5 Miles from Wallingford, a good situation for a Tavern, one having been formerly kept there. For Particulars enquire of Samuel Tracket, of North-Haven.

INOCULATION.

IN Consequence of a Vote of the Town of Say-Brook, and by Permission from the Civil Authority and Select-Men, the Subscriber has opened an Hospital in the second Parish in said Town, for the Purpose of communicating the Small-Pox by Inoculation; his first Class are now going out, and the Hospital ready for the Reception of more Patients.—Gentlemen or Ladies who incline to favour him with their Custom, may depend on being faithfully attended, by their Humble Servant,

ELISHA ELY.

Say-Brook, April 11, 1781. (2)

DRAUGHT HORSES, *wanted by* MICHAEL TODD; *for which West India Goods, or paper money will be given. New Haven, April* 12.

I AM appointed by His Excellency Governor Trumbull, to muster and inspect the Men and Arms for the two Battalions raised for the Defence of the Post at Horse Neck. The Towns which have not furnish'd their Quotas are requested to forward them to this Place as soon as possible, as they are much wanted on the Lines.—It is General Waterbury's positive Order that the Officers for the two Battalions immediately join.

ELI LEAVENWORTH.

New-Haven, April 9, 1781.

WE the Subscribers being (by the Honorable Court of Probate for the District of New-London) appointed Commissioners, to receive and examine the Claims o the Creditors on the Estate of Nathaniel Peck, late of Lyme, in the County of New-London, deceased, represented insolvent:—

The advertisement headed "TO BE SOLD" shows probably the first commercial use of Buell's type, in the *Connecticut Journal* for April 19, 1781.

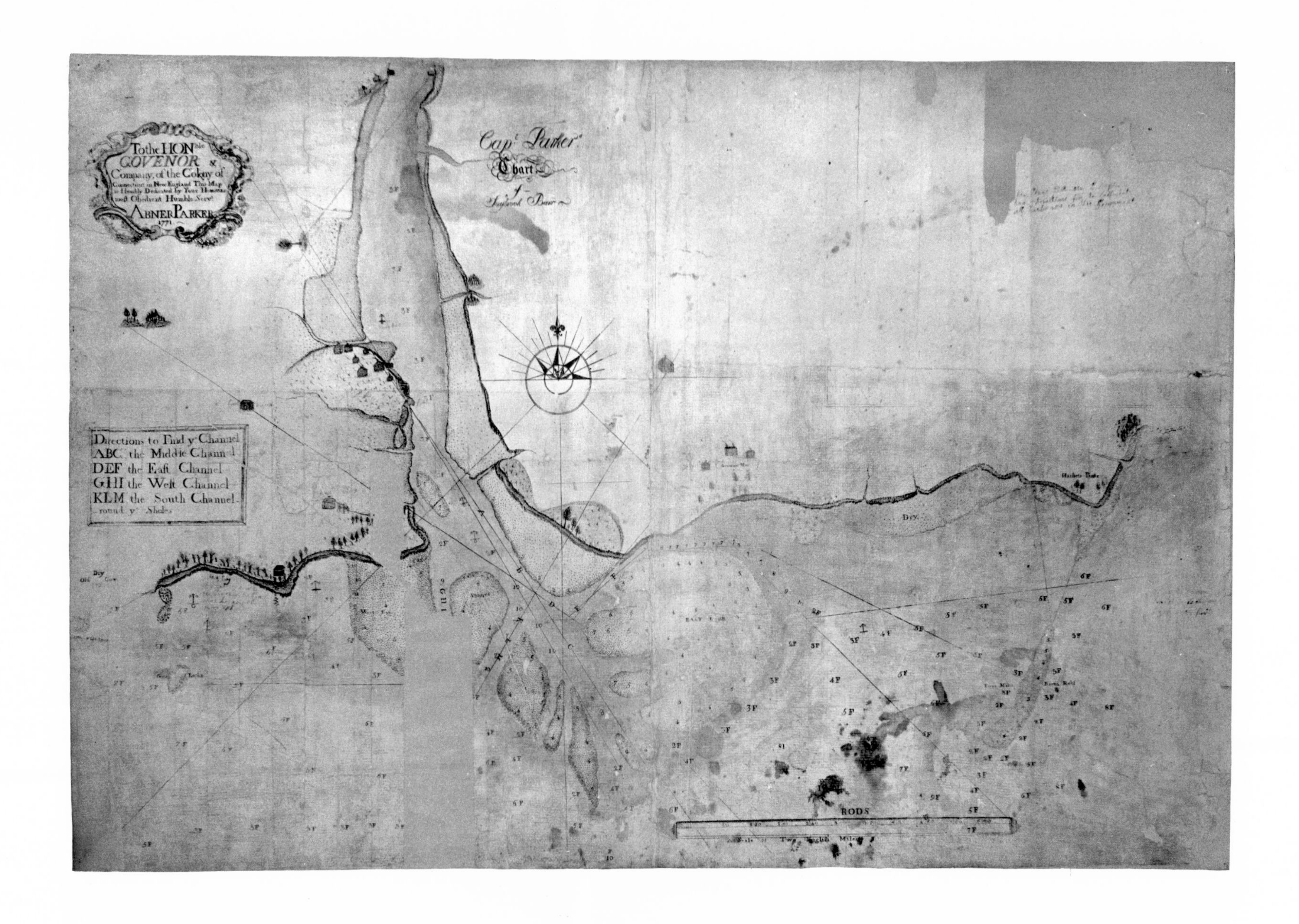

Abner Parker's "Chart of Saybrook Barr" engraved by Abel Buell. From the only known copy, in the Connecticut Historical Society. The reproduction shows the actual condition of the print.

The First Connecticut Engraver

IT has been said in an earlier chapter that Buell's accomplishment in the silversmith's craft was without especial significance. He was not the first man known to us who found his chief interest in life to lie in activities subsidiary to his ostensible business, and who, one must add, rendered service to his fellows by a persistent neglect of the work for which he had been trained. Even though he stood outside the main current of progress in the industry that he initiated but failed to establish in this country, his experiments and his partial success in type founding have the peculiar interest of priority in the history of that essential craft in America. In the art of engraving, his achievement is even less well known than in his other forms of expression, but I believe it can be shown that in this art his service was of such a character as to be worthy of memory, that in a sense it was more distinctive than his fabrication of the precious metals, and that it possessed, furthermore, an importance to his contemporaries as great as his imperfectly realized plans for the founding of type.

THE "CHART OF SAYBROOK BARR"

Buell the engraver makes his entrance into our story in connection with a project that lay close to the interests of an important Connecticut community. In October, 1770, the inhabitants of the Connecticut River towns moved themselves to the task of making their waterway easier of entrance from the Sound.[55] To this end they petitioned the Assembly for permission to raise by lottery the money needed for the execution of their plans. In May, 1772, the Assembly gave them leave to organize their lottery scheme and appointed a committee for its management with Matthew Talcott as chairman. The resolution further provided that the lottery should not be set up until June 6, 1773.[56] We need speak here only of such details of the history of the Connecticut River Lottery as relate it to the story of Abel Buell.

In the initial memorial of the Connecticut River folk, in October, 1770, occurs a sentence which connects their navigation project with the activities of our engraver. One of the statements made by the petitioners was that "a complete chart or map [of the mouth of the river] hath been lately made by Captain Abner Parker of Saybrook." In the order of the Assembly which met in May, 1772, it was provided that of the £337 to be raised the sum of £37 was to be paid directly to Captain Abner Parker. A resolution of the Assembly of October, 1774, advances the story. It is in these words:[57]

Upon the Memorial of Abner Parker of Saybrook, shewing to this Assembly that a Lottery was granted for improving and rendering more usefull the navigation at the mouth of Connecticut River which hath been drawn, and a Comittee appointed to carry said design into Execution, That the said Parker by advice of said Comittee & sundry other Persons hath procured a plate, & caused the same to be properly engraved to render the Knowledge of the Navigation of s^d^ River most extensive & usefull, praying that said Comittie may be enabled & enjoined to pay to him the Expence of procuring & engraving s^d^ plate out of the monies raised by s^d^ Lottery &c as ℘ memorial on file dated the 25th day of October AD. 1774.

Resolved by this Assembly that said Comittie may and shall pay to s^d^ Abner Parker out of the monies in their hands raised by said Lottery the sum of Thirty Six pounds five Shillings lawfull money being the Amount of the Expence of procuring and

engraving the Plate aforesaid, and that the same shall be allowed them on their account of the Expenditure of the monies aforesaid.
Oct. 1774

Parker doubtless attached to his memorial as an exhibit the bill which is now found in the state archives accompanying the resolution of Assembly that has just been quoted. This document brings us at last upon an episode of interest in the history of American engraving:[58]

Octr 1774
Capt Abner Parker D^r To Abel Buell

To 2 Large Copper Plates	£6.5.0.
To Ingraving 2 Large Copper Plates	30.0.0.
	£36.5.0

As the result of these transactions in the Assembly we have a fairly complete history of the first engraving of any consequence made in the colony of Connecticut. It is certain, one may say, that the committee intended from the beginning to cause Captain Parker's chart to be engraved, and that in May, 1772, they included the odd sum of £37 in the amount to be derived from the lottery as payment for the engraver. It is likely that the amount so specified was the result of an estimate by Buell, who would have been consulted in advance as to the cost of the plate and of the engraving. It is difficult otherwise to explain the presence in the main sum of that specific amount.

The title and description of the chart are as follows:

[*Title in upper left center in script and black letter:*]

Capt Parker^s Chart of Saybrook Barr

[*At upper left, in a cartouche, with delicately engraved flower and ribbon border, in roman letter:*]

To the HON^ble GOVENOR & Company, of the Colony of Connecticut in New England This Map is Humbly Dedicated by Your Honours most Obedient Humble Serv[t] ABNER PARKER 1771.

[*Beneath, in box, six lines in roman letter:*]

Directions to Find y[e] Channel . . .

The print, made from two plates, measures 26¾ x 39⅜ inches. The margins have been trimmed away in the only known copy, a reproduction of which faces page 57.

Here is one commission that Buell did not fumble. The engraving of the plate was carried through successfully and competently, and, in October, 1774, the bill for the work was submitted to the Colony. A statement by Captain Abner Parker, later to be quoted, assured the Assembly that the chart printed from it, the only known specimen of which is before us, was for years thereafter put by local pilots to the use for which it had been intended.

The workmanship of the engraving is so sure and clear that one can hardly think of it as the earliest work of the engraver's burin even though it is the earliest which can be dated. Two other examples of Buell's work, a Yale diploma form and a writing sheet, *The Sequel of Arts and Sciences,* must also be regarded as having been engraved before his departure from New Haven in December, 1774. The evidence of competency displayed in these prints and the Saybrook Chart is so great as to predicate an apprenticeship of some duration to the engraver's craft. We have not far to look in our search for the when and where of that apprenticeship. In the preceding chapter, line engraving—the making of an incised design—was described as a procedure in the customary operations of the goldsmith. The engraver's prints from his incised, or intaglio, plates are first cousins of the proofs—rubbings or lightly inked impressions—taken by the goldsmith to preserve a pattern of the ornamental design, the coat of arms, or the monogram he had chased upon the surface of an important production. It must be that we owe the skill of Buell, the engraver, to the teachings of his master, Ebenezer Chittenden, active and successful silversmith of Madison and New Haven.

The circumstance that the date engraved on the Saybrook Chart is three years earlier than the date of Buell's bill for payment seems to require explanation. The chart was drawn by Abner Parker as early as 1770, and when the petition from the river towns was preferred to the Assembly for a second time in the following year it is not unlikely that it was accompanied as an exhibit of intention by a manuscript copy of the map with the complimentary dedication dated 1771. The lottery was authorized in May, 1772, with the provision that it was not to be set up until June, 1773, so that no money could have been in hand from the percentage on the sale of tickets until some months after this date. It is not characteristic of committees in cases of this sort to incur considerable expenses until money is in hand or in view, and I believe that this committee waited until money began to come in from the lottery before they authorized Buell to proceed with the engraving. In this case the date of the plate would be late in 1773 or early in 1774. The bill for it, as we have seen, was not submitted until October, 1774.

We have the assurance of Captain Parker that the chart was a useful aid to navigators. In a memorial to the Assembly of 1788, he rehearses that he had "procured a Regular [Plan] according to the Order and Direction afores^{d} Struck off on a Copper Plate engrav^{d} from Sounding & Mensuration for that purpose which he humbly conceives has been and will Continue to be of Eminent Service to Those who use the Navigation of Connec^{t} River."[59] This may be the prejudiced testimony of the person chiefly interested, but it was a claim presented to the Assembly in the hope of securing recompense for the service thus described. We may think of this chart as forming for many years part of the equipment of ships engaged in the New England coasting trade.

As in the case of most maps intended for use under circumstances of peculiar rudeness, almost the whole edition of this mariner's chart has been worn out of existence. There remains, as far as is known, only one copy of the original print. This is in the library of the Connecticut Historical Society. A very skillful tracing of it was reproduced by the heliotype process and published in the *Public Records of the Colony of Connecticut,* volume thirteen, page 503. The Connecticut Historical Society copy, however, is not in the form of a print made from the earliest state of the plate. The present custodian of the chart, Mr. Thompson Harlow, writes as follows concerning it:[60] "East of the River is a building labelled 'Governor's House,' the home of Matthew Griswold who was Governor 1784–1786. Since this information could not have been added to the plate until the election in May, 1784, this state of the chart must have been printed after that time." Such evidence as this of continued interest in the chart bears out Captain Parker's assurance to the Assembly in 1788 that the engraved chart "has been and will Continue to be of Eminent Service to Those who use the Navigation of Connec^{t} River."

THE YALE DIPLOMA FORM

In our biographical summary we quoted part of an advertisement of September 2, 1777, in which Captain Bernard Romans reminded the young gentlemen of Yale College that by applying to Mrs. Buell those about to receive their degrees might be supplied with "blank diplomas, neatly printed on the very best of Imperial paper." These words referred to the diploma form engraved by Abel Buell which we are now about to describe. As its maker at the time of the announcement had not yet returned to New

Haven from his exile, one makes the assumption that the diploma must have been a production of the period before his departure thence in December, 1774. That assumption is confirmed as fact by the copy formerly owned by the late George Dudley Seymour, dated September 14, 1774, and filled in with the name of Thomas Welles. It was probably, indeed, one of his earliest ventures into the field of copper-plate engraving, and if we may judge by Mrs. Buell's ability to supply it in September, 1777, and the preservation in the Yale University Library of a specimen of it filled in with the name of William Spalding on September 9, 1778, it remained for some time a staple of his shop.

The diploma print may be described as follows:

[*Engraved emblematical design at top, as in reproduction facing page 80, followed by heading:*]

Praeses et Socii Collegii Yalensis Novo Portu Connecticutensium Omnibus has literas . . .

[*Nine lines of text, the whole surrounded by an engraved Chippendale border. At lower right, outside the border:*]

A. Buell Sculp.

The sheet in the Henry Daggett copy measures 11¾ by 13¾ inches; the plate measures 9½ by 10½ inches.

Our reproduction of the Buell diploma shows that the design and execution resemble somewhat the florid style of the engrosser of formal documents. Buell presumably had studied his Bickham's *Universal Penman,* and here was trying out alphabets and decorative elements illustrated in that comprehensive assortment of styles. The composition exhibits a quality of exuberance which if carried a bit further would have given the production an appearance of fussiness not fitted to the purpose it was intended to serve. The Yale diplomas of the present day are very much more pleasing and more appropriate to the stately language in which their matter is enshrined. The eighteenth century could go very wrong in matters of taste. The piece serves admirably, however, as an evidence of its engraver's versatility and of the mastery he had obtained over his tools and materials.

THE WRITING SHEET

The most important of the Buell engravings are the maps of Saybrook Bar and the United States; the most pleasing is the decorated writing sheet already briefly mentioned as a production of the period before his departure from New Haven for Florida. We may now describe that piece more fully in the following terms:

The Sequel of Arts and Sciences

[*Decorated blank form on a single sheet with imprint at bottom center outside the engraved design:*]

Printed for & Sold by the Proprietors A. B. and J. R. in New Haven.

The sheet measures 17⅛ x 13¾ inches; the plate measures 16⅛ x 13 inches.

A print of this description and title is described by Mantle Fielding in his "Supplement" to D. M. N. Stauffer, *American Engravers upon Copper and Steel* as the work of Amos Doolittle. Mr. Fielding misread A. B. in the imprint for A. D. Some years ago a copy of the print was purchased by the New York Historical Society and identified, so far as may be evidenced by time, place, initials, and circumstances, as the work of Abel Buell, published in partnership with the New York printer, James Rivington. Another copy of the print, that one from which our reproduction (facing page 64) is made, was soon afterwards discovered among the possessions of the Connecticut Historical Society.[61]

In the endearing form of the needlework sampler, the colonial maiden displayed the degree of skill she had attained in the household arts of stitching and embroidery. This was her masterpiece, affirming the end of her apprenticeship. Skill in penmanship was a goal analogous to this in the life of the colonial boy. His attainment of competence in that field was frequently memorialized by a display of his best writing and lettering upon a single sheet, in a blank book of several pages, or sometimes, as we learn from the piece before us, upon an elaborately engraved single sheet of impressive size. But to do this, we also learn, was not the prerogative of boys alone; girls might challenge them in their own field. A boy would scorn the making of a sampler, but a girl might make a display of her handwriting ability. The Buell writing sheet in the Connecticut Historical Society was filled in at Norwich in Mr. Kinne's school by Matthew Talcott, Jr., but the specimen of it in the New York Historical Society was the work of a forward young lady of eight years, Susannah Darling of New Haven.

The large blank area reserved for the writing display in the center of *The Sequel of Arts and Sciences* is surrounded by a compartmented engraved border showing the tools and operations of the arts and crafts of Limning, Engraving, Printing, Hat Making, Husbandry, Botany, Glass Grinding, and Mechanicks. These were not original designs by Buell but copies or adaptations engraved by him after the illustrations of one of the current English books of crafts and trades. In his discussion of *The Sequel,* Mr. Thompson Harlow has identified one of these sources as Volumes II and III of *The Universal Magazine of Knowledge and Pleasure,* of London, 1748. The engravings on the Buell sheet are interesting to the antiquarian primarily as the work of an American-born craftsman of the colonial period, but their competence provides for them a sounder claim to esteem than that which is based upon the merely quaint and primitive. The design of the sheet and its execution add to the good opinion we hold of the work accomplished by the earliest Connecticut engraver.

THE BUELL-RIVINGTON-ROMANS ASSOCIATION

It may be concluded from its imprint that *The Sequel of Arts and Sciences* provides us with evidence of that business association between Abel Buell and James Rivington which in our first chapter we suggested had been brought about through transactions connected with engraving. It is a sound assumption that the A. B. and J. R. of the imprint were Buell and Rivington, and the inference may be drawn that if the two men were associated in this single project they may well have been associated in others. It is difficult otherwise than by such an inference to account for the claim of 500 pounds York money which in 1775 Rivington brought against Buell in the New Haven County Court. In our endeavor to explain this evidence of extensive dealings between the two men we bring a third person into our consideration of the problem. The Buell-Rivington relationship becomes more complicated but more interesting when, upon evidence which is scarcely more substantial than a feeling of atmosphere, we add to it the person of Bernard Romans, the Dutch engineer and cartographer whom we have already met in the act of befriending Aletta Buell when, at the time her husband was still in exile, she badly needed help and encouragement.

It has been said more than once upon the basis of John Warner Barber's article (see our note 2), often referred to in this work, that Buell was employed by Bernard Romans to engrave or assist in engraving certain of the maps which bear Romans's name. This we believe to be true, but we cannot go along with Barber when he says further that Romans employed Buell to survey and map for him the

Pensacola area for a map of North America which he constructed sometime after 1770.[62] There is, to begin with, no evidence that Romans then or ever made a map of North America. It is probable that in the growth of the tradition recorded by Barber confusion occurred between the great Florida charts made by Romans and published by him in 1775 and the *Map of the United States* made and published by Buell in 1784. But whatever underlay the tradition of a Pensacola survey by Buell, certain stubborn evidence offered by the calendar compels us to relinquish it. Buell did not leave New Haven for Pensacola until sometime in December, 1774. Romans left Florida in February, 1773,[63] and entered almost at once upon a busy life of writing, engraving, map making, and publication in Pennsylvania, New York, and New England. In an advertisement in the *New York Gazetteer* of February 10, 1774, Romans says that he was then in expectation of assistance from his friend George Gauld for surveys of the East part of West Florida.[64] Evidently he did not have long to wait, for on October 20, 1774, he announced that the engraving of all the plates for the charts had been completed.[65] This announcement, it is to be observed and emphasized, was made some two months before Buell left New Haven for Pensacola in December, 1774. In the face of it we must discard as untenable the tradition that Buell made a maritime survey of Pensacola Bay and Harbor for the Romans charts of 1775. We must seek another explanation of the tradition that a relationship existed between Romans and Buell.

It is clear from the contemporary documentation, provided by P. Lee Phillips in his study of Bernard Romans, that the Dutch engineer not only received help in the making of the marine surveys embodied in his Florida charts, but that from the beginning of the process of publication he hired assistance in the actual engraving of the nine plates which made up the complex work, the largest engraving project of any kind accomplished in colonial America. It has been suggested, and there is abundant precedent in European practice to justify the suggestion, that the presence of his name upon the charts—"B. Romans inv. delin. & in Aere incidit" and "B Romans inv^{t} et sculp^{t} 1774"—made claim only to the engraving of the cartouches beneath which these legends are found. He had, in fact, made no concealment of his dependence upon the services of skilled engravers. In his first printed announcement of the work in a broadside (of which there is a copy in the John Carter Brown Library), headed *Proposals for Printing by Subscription . . . ,* dated "Philadelphia, August 5, 1773," he informs prospective subscribers that "a masterly engraver is now employed on the Work at New York, and in six Weeks from this Date, it is hoped a sheet shall be made public." He goes on to assure his readers that he would not be asking part payment in advance but for the fact that he "presumed on the Works being actually begun . . ." In a later paragraph he returns to the matter of engraving, offering to show on request the agreement which called for his payment to the New York engraver the sum of "£3 14 s for every 48 hours he works thereon." Five months later in an advertisement in the *Boston Gazette* for January 10, 1774, he wrote in his appeal for support of the project: "A great Part of the Work is already printed . . ." Read in context, this statement almost certainly refers to the Florida maps rather than to *A Concise History of East and West Florida,* the book which is mentioned later in the advertisement as something to be added to the maps. But certainty that the engraving of the maps was carried on steadily in 1773 and 1774 is found in the terms of a promissory note given by Romans in connection with his purchase of two hogsheads of rum. In this note of "New York 10 Augt 1774," for the sum of £27 5*s* 1*d,* he pledged as security for payment "all and every my

Effects especially the Copperplates of my work."[66] Evidently progress upon the engraving of the maps had been of such a character that the plates completed by that time might be counted a considerable part of his personal estate.

A final assurance that Romans employed professional engravers in the prosecution of the work upon the Florida charts is found in the account books of Paul Revere, of Boston, wherein charges are entered against Captain Bernard Romans, dated May 4, July 9, and October 21, 1774, for plates of "a map of East Florida," "part of a map of Florida," and a third plate, contents not specified, which doubtless was also one of the Florida series.[67] These plates charged for by Revere as the work of May, July, and October, 1774, must have been the last of the Florida chart plates to be engraved. On October 20th of that year, as already said, Romans announced that the engraving of all the plates had been completed.

The Revere connection with the Romans charts combined with the August, 1773, reference to the employment of an engraver upon the project in New York makes it sufficiently clear that the engraving of the charts could have been the work of at least two men in two different places. If that was the case more than two men of more than two places might have been employed, and the hand of Abel Buell of New Haven added to those of Paul Revere and the unknown craftsman in New York. It is believed that the printing of the charts was carried out in the large, well-equipped printing shop of James Rivington, of New York. It is a matter of certain knowledge that Romans and Rivington were closely associated in this period, and of equally certain knowledge that at this time Buell and Rivington were well known to each other. Rivington would have known that the New Haven engraver at some time in the period 1772–1774 had been employed (or was still employed) in engraving the plate for the chart of Saybrook Bar, and might appropriately have recommended him to Romans for similar work upon the Florida charts.[68]

The probability of an association of Buell with Romans through their common acquaintance with Rivington is not confined wholly to his possible participation in the production of the Florida charts. It is generally believed that the Romans book, *A Concise Natural History of East and West Florida,* published in April, 1775, came from the press of Rivington, though Mr. P. Lee Phillips, the biographer of Romans, upon what seems to be unsubstantial grounds, maintained a contrary view.[69] This book contains three small harbor charts—*Pensacola Bar, Mobile Bar,* and *Entrances of Tampa Bay.* These are delicately and competently engraved, and such place names as they bear are in the general style of roman lettering found in Buell's *Chart of Saybrook Bar* and *Map of the United States,* though the separate letters in many cases are not identical in form. Lack of genuine evidence forbids us to claim these small maps as the work of Buell, but it is not improper that they should be mentioned as among the prints which he might possibly have made through his association with James Rivington. A slightly more solid case may be made for his proposed participation in another aspect of the illustration of the book through a close reading of the notice which Romans himself added to its last leaf. The first paragraph of the notice reads:

> The map of the country of the savage nations, intended to be put, facing page 72, was engraved by a Gentleman who resides in the country 60 or 70 miles from New-York, to whom the plate was sent; but when it was sent back, it miscarried, through the carelesness of the waggoner; and though the publication has been delayed some time on that account, it is not yet come to hand; the reader will therefore please to expect said map with the second volume.

I do not wish to attach too great weight to this tenuous thread of connection between Buell and Romans, but neither do I like to ignore its existence. There were not many copperplate engravers in America at this time, and even fewer who lived "60 or 70 miles from New York." Abel Buell was a copperplate engraver who dwelt at New Haven, some sixty-odd miles by road from New York, and if it be objected that a residence in New Haven could not properly be spoken of as a residence "in the country" one need only reply that these words were written by a denizen of New York City. The proposed second volume of the Romans book was never published, so that neither corroboration nor disproof of my suggestion may be looked for in that quarter.

Whatever may be the true state of this case, it is certain that a relationship existed between Buell and Romans at a period subsequent to the publication of the Florida maps even if it cannot be shown that it had an earlier beginning. We encountered Romans in New Haven in 1777 in the act of befriending Aletta Buell. Two years later we find Abel Buell, who, incidentally, was not a bookseller, named among others in New Haven who have for sale Romans's *Annals of the Troubles in the Netherlands*.[70] If this slender but definite evidence of an association between them be added to the tradition that Buell engraved plates for Romans and to that sum of knowledge be joined the conjectures made in the foregoing paragraphs, we may find ourselves becoming convinced that some of the work issued by Bernard Romans was in reality Buell's, just as we know that other parts of it pertained to Paul Revere. After all, except that they gave Buell credit for the actual survey of Pensacola, this is what the older writers said, and the end of the argument is only to confirm the element of truth in the tradition.

THE ARMS OF THE STATE

It is not generally known that the arms of Connecticut which appear on the title page of the compiled laws of the state in 1784 and at the head of the printed session laws for many years afterwards were from plates engraved by Abel Buell, but there seems to be good reason for believing this to be the case. Following the publication in 1784 of the *Acts and Laws of the State of Connecticut in America,* as the title of the compilation reads, the printer, Timothy Green of New London, submitted an account to the Assembly in which are found these two charges:[71]

To Abel Buell's Bill for engraving the State Arms	2. 0. 0.
To cash paid for Copper for the same	0. 4. 0.

Any copy of this compilation, of either the first or second edition, will be found to contain on its title page a relief cut of the state arms. On the evidence of the printer's statement to the Assembly, we can feel justified in ascribing this plate to the hand of Abel Buell, even though it is unsigned and without distinguishing characteristics.

For lack of a more definite designation the cut may be given the following made-up title:

The Arms of the State of Connecticut

[*Relief cut with shield charged with three emblematic grape-laden vines, motto "Qui tra sus"; in surrounding frame, "Sigill. Reip. Connecticutensis," the whole within a floriated border.*]

The cut measures 2⅜ x 2⅛ inches.

With this brief statement of its principal features our discussion of the arms cut might be supposed to end, but there is more to be said about it. Thomas and Samuel Green, printers of New Haven, were likewise in the business of occasionally printing for the government. They, too,

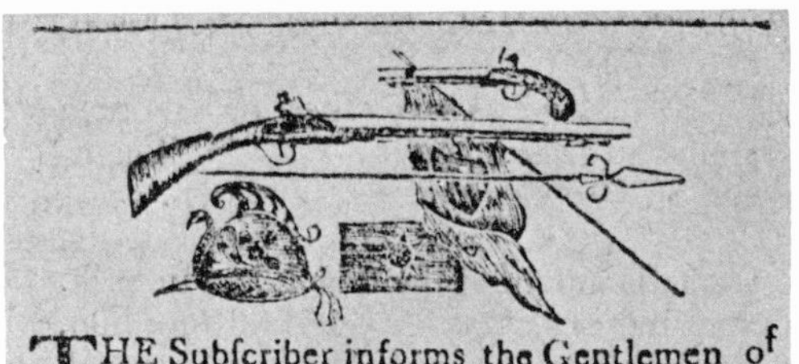

THE Subſcriber informs the Gentlemen of this City and the adjacent country, that he has a good apparatus for repairing, cleaning, and poliſhing their Military arms of every deſcription, and will thank them for their cuſtom this ſeaſon—he makes the moſt approved and faſhionable ornaments for Military Caps, and Cartridge-Boxes; paints and gilds Flags; engraves Seals, Dies, Punches, and Copper Plates, marks Silver Plate and Rings, with elegant Cyphers and Arms; cuts Blocks and ornaments for Printers; makes and repairs any common or difficult work, fabricated from metal or wood. The ſmalleſt favors will be gratefully acknowledged by their humble ſerv't.

ABEL BUEL.

Hartford, April 16.

Buell's advertisement in the *American Mercury,* Hartford, for April 16, 1801. The block was probably cut by Buell himself.

First plate Second plate

The Arms of Connecticut

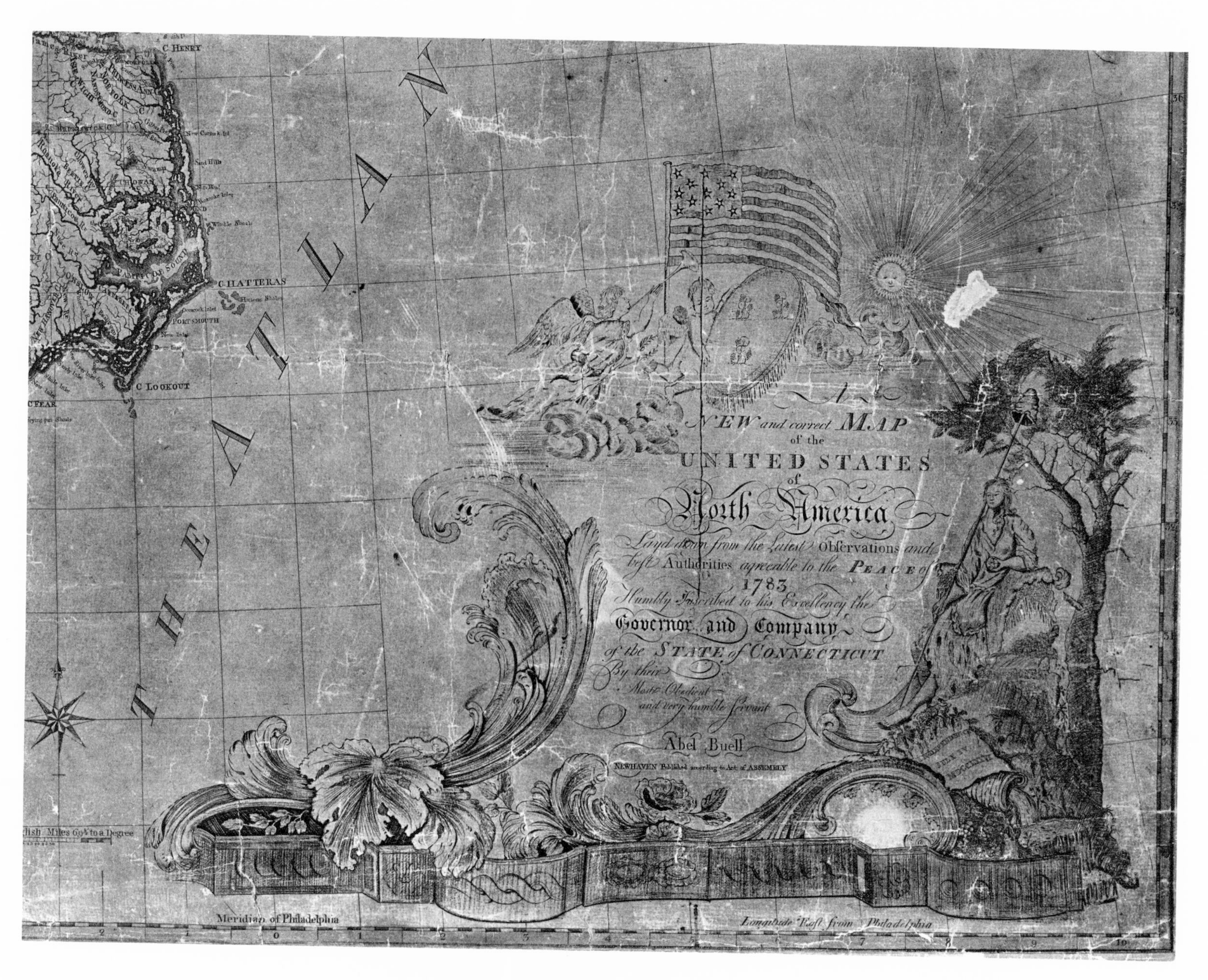

The cartouche, much reduced, of Buell's most elaborate work of engraving, the great wall map of the United States, 1784. Reproduced from the Yale University Library copy.

would want a cut of the arms to use in that work. Accordingly a replica of the arms as originally made for their brother, Timothy Green of New London, was cut, or possibly, cast, for Thomas and Samuel of New Haven. The lower corners of the replica, through carelessness or faulty method of reproduction, show slight differences from the original design. Print (a) in our accompanying illustration (facing page 72) shows the original cut as made for and used by Timothy Green of New London; print (b) is from the cut made for and used by Thomas and Samuel Green of New Haven. By taking account of the differences between the two it is possible to employ them in bibliographical investigation and attribute correctly to each of the Green establishments certain editions of the Connecticut session laws which appeared after 1784 without name of printer or place of publication.[72]

In examining one of the pages embellished by Buell's cut of the Connecticut arms, one quickly appreciates the sympathy that exists between its printed and engraved portions. Too often an intaglio copperplate engraving printed in conjunction with type seems an intrusion, but Buell's relief cut harmonizes admirably with its typographical setting.

THE MAP OF THE UNITED STATES

We come now to a consideration of Buell's most ambitious work with the graver. In the *Connecticut Journal* for March 31, 1784, appeared the following notice:

BUEL'S MAP

Of the United States of America, Laid down from the latest observations and best authorities, agreeable to the peace of 1783, is now published, and ready for subscribers.

As this Map is the effect of the compiler's long and unwearied application, diligence and industry, and as perfection has been the great object of his labours, and it being the first ever compiled, engraved, and finished by one man, and an

American, he flatters himself, that every patriotic gentleman, and lover of geographical knowledge, will not hesitate to encourage the improvement of his own country. Every favour will be most gratefully acknowledged, by the public's Most obediant and very humble servant,

ABEL BUEL

New-Haven, March 31, 1784.

We know very little about the circumstances of publication of the map described for the first time in this advertisement, nor do we know the extent of its circulation and usefulness. There seem to remain no contemporary references to it. It is not known how many copies were issued, nor is there a record of its cost to subscribers. Such information as we possess concerning it is derived from the announcement that has been quoted and from the map itself, of which there remain copies in the Connecticut Historical Society, the Yale University Library (formerly the American Geographical Society copy), and the New York Public Library.

The title and description of the map may be given as follows:

[*In a decorative cartouche here reproduced:*]

A New and correct Map of the United States of North America Layd down from the Latest Observations and best Authorities agreeable to the PEACE of 1783 Humbly Inscribed to his Excellency the Governor and Company of the State of Connecticut By their Most Obedient and very humble Servant Abel Buell Newhaven Published according to Act of Assembly

Printed probably on four sheets, the map measures overall 41 x 46.5 inches. The copy of the map in the New York Public Library (Stokes Collection) lacks the imprint and thus seems to be of an earlier issue than the others located above.

The imprint of the map, "Newhaven Published according to Act of Assembly," bears a special significance for the bibliographer and historian. In consequence of a memorial presented by John Ledyard, author of *A Journal of Captain Cook's Last Voyage,* Hartford, 1783, the Connecticut Assembly in January, 1783, passed a general law for the protection of literary property, the earliest copyright law to appear upon the statute books of an American state. I have discussed this notable Connecticut act and its significance in H. Lehmann-Haupt, *The Book in America,* second edition, New York, 1952, pages 102–106. Buell was now, in March, 1784, seeking the protection of its terms. His phrase, "Published according to Act of Assembly," is one of the very earliest claims to copyright to be printed in or upon an issue of the press of the United States.

In Buell's "Map of the United States" we find that which compels admiration for the enterprise and industry of the engraver, if not invariably for his skill. It is a large map, measuring 41 x 46.5 inches, intended evidently for use as a wall map. This fact may account for the rarity of copies of the work, for it is the wall maps, exposed as they are to dust, to dampness, and to the action of the sun's rays, that soonest fade and become useless and uninteresting objects to their possessors. Their size and the dinginess that they acquire with time predestine them, once they are outmoded, to the trash heap and the fire. In this case the appearance not long afterwards of more accurate and more skillfully executed maps of the United States tended early to bring the Buell map into disregard as a production once serviceable but soon lacking in consequence.

One of the interesting features of the map is the elaborate cartouche found in its lower right-hand corner. It is reproduced here as an example of the pictorial skill of the artist, a display of thoughtfulness in design and fluidity and vigor in execution. The upper portion of the design contains the American flag with its thirteen stars and stripes beneath which are two cherubs, one lustily acclaiming the emblem with a trumpet, the other bearing a fringed tambour frame on which are displayed the three grape-laden vines of the arms of Connecticut. To the right of the flag, the sun, with a human face and a bold radiation proceeding from a ruff that surrounds it, looks down benignly upon the picture that forms the right-hand border of the cartouche. This comprises a sturdy tree beneath which, rock-enthroned, sits the figure of Liberty, holding in the right hand a staff surmounted by the Liberty cap and in the left a globe on which can be read the word "America." Beneath her feet on an open ground are engraved the words:

INDEPENDENCE
JULY IV
MDCCLXXVI

Flowing horns of plenty, a low conventionalized wall as a base and an involuted design of foliage form the bottom and left-hand borders of the design, with the long title and dedication filling the central space of the cartouche.

THE SOURCES OF BUELL'S MAP

In the discussion of any early map one is normally interested in the sources from which it is derived. Happy is the investigator who holds in his hands a map in which new and striking information has been embodied as the result of the designer's exploration or the explorations of others not previously given graphic record. There is no such emotion to be experienced by one who examines the Buell map of the United States, for that cartographical document is made up from printed maps which for a long time had been available to all who had need for them. It was the second- and third-hand compilation that its maker claimed it to be and nothing more.

It proves to be difficult to designate any single map as the prototype of the Buell production. The most notable eighteenth-century representation of the British possessions in North America was unquestionably the huge wall map constructed from original surveys by John Mitchell for the Lords Commissioners for Trade and Plantations, *A Map of the British and French Dominions in North America,* first published in London in 1755. Thereafter successive editions in English, French, and German made the Mitchell map everywhere the most familiar delineation of North America from Florida to Labrador, and from the Atlantic to a point on the western plains some seven degrees beyond the meridian of the Lake of the Woods, the frequently cited reference point in what is today the Minnesota-Manitoba area. The ultimate distinction of the Mitchell map was its employment in 1783 by the Peace Commissioners in laying down the boundaries of the new United States. To name the derivatives of Mitchell's memorable publication would be to load this page with a catalogue of map titles comprising most of the best-known representations of North America of the second half of the century. There is little question that the Buell map of 1784, drawing, probably, for certain of its features upon one of the three English editions of Mitchell of the years 1773–75, would be listed among these derivatives. The general geographic scope of the map, the configuration of its coast lines, and the coastal place names it employs point strongly toward the Mitchell map as one of its important sources. The names and locations of several of the Indian nations found upon the Buell map are distinctly, even to their spellings, those of Mitchell. The tenor of certain legends, the unusual spellings and misspellings of some of the place names, offer revealing evidence of a relationship between the two productions. Even their respective cartouches display a similarity in the nature and disposition of symbolic elements and, more subtly, the presence in each of a rhythmical feeling, an easy fluidity in design and composition, which has already been remarked upon in describing this feature of the Buell production.

A close examination of the Buell map assures one, however, that it contains much data not found in the Mitchell prototype, data which, indeed, may have been drawn from several additional sources. We content ourselves here with the consideration of one of these sources which has been identified beyond reasonable doubt as having provided a principal contribution to Buell's knowledge. The process of identification has led us to matter of special interest in the field of American historical cartography.

A brilliant and admirable figure of the American scene in the days of the French and Indian War and the Revolution was the New Jersey born engineer officer in the British service, Captain Thomas Hutchins, of the Royal American Regiment. In 1780 after an irksome imprisonment, Hutchins resigned his commission and left England for America by way of France to join and support the cause of his countrymen. He was soon to become by title and in fact "Geographer to the United States." Here we are concerned only with his earlier work, *A New Map of the Western Parts of Virginia, Pennsylvania, Maryland and North Carolina,* London, 1778, constructed by him upon the basis of his own surveys and those of a number of associates—engineers, cartographers, and frontiersmen—to whom, in the preface of his book soon to be mentioned, he allots full and generously expressed recognition. Among the cartographers was Lewis Evans, whose map of 1755 and accompanying *Geographical Essays* supplemented, especially for the areas east of the Alleghanies, Hutchins's own surveys and observations. Accompanying the Hutchins map of 1778 was a book descriptive of its contents. *A Topographical Description of Virginia, Pennsylvania, Maryland, and North Carolina* revealed the fair face of the land beyond the Alleghanies to a world of land-hungry individuals and enterprising land companies held temporarily in leash by the War from the great westward surge soon to occur. His portrayal and discussion of the Ohio and Mississippi basins—navigable rivers and lesser waterways, fertile intervales, high plateaus, great hardwood forests, salt licks, cane brakes—presented in the measured accents of truth, offered incitement to the young and aggressive to cross the ranges to a new land of promise.

It was to this map and this book that Buell went for much of the detail recorded in the trans-Alleghany area of his own production. Though his assimilation of its data was far from thorough, and its transference superficially accomplished, he yet observed faithfully and carried over to his own map certain features of unusual interest. Among these was a natural phenomenon of the Cherokee—or Tennessee—River, that broad, slowly descending series of rapids, thirty-five miles in length, which we know as "Muscle Shoals," and which, we believe, was first designated by that name in print in the Hutchins book and map of 1778. That feature of the Hutchins works Buell embodied in his own production, and with it a minor phenomenon of the same river which Hutchins called "The Whirl or Suck." So far as I have been able to determine, Buell could not have found these designations in any other book or map. His use of these place names would, if I am correct, offer evidence of his dependence upon Hutchins even if to them could not be added an impressive list of place names and descriptive legends derived from the same source. It has been said mistakenly that the name "Muscle Shoals" made its first appearance in print on the Joseph Purcell map of the United States in Morse's *American Geography* of 1789,[73] but we have seen that it had been employed by Buell in 1784 upon the basis of its use by Thomas Hutchins in his book and map of 1778.

In the general area of today's northern Alabama, Buell

engraved upon his map the place name "Hutchins camp," using a term and making an allusion I have found in neither the Hutchins book nor the Hutchins map we have been discussing. This circumstance suggests knowledge on Buell's part drawn from other writings, printed or manuscript, of Hutchins, or even permits the supposition of their personal acquaintance. Such an association is far from improbable. Buell was resident in Pensacola in 1775 and part if not all of 1776. Hutchins was stationed in Pensacola with his battalion of the Royal Americans, employed in building barracks, exploring, observing, and writing from 1772 to 1777. Buell had already been concerned in the engraving of a map or maps. Hutchins, the engineer and map maker, was the sort of person whose acquaintance he would have sought, and in that small community would, it seems, successfully have made.

It can be said of Buell that when he described his map as based upon the "best Authorities" he was speaking the literal truth. In drawing upon the solid labors of Mitchell, Hutchins, and Lewis Evans, Buell was traveling first class in the very best company of his time and place.

GENERAL CONSIDERATION OF THE BUELL MAP

When we come to consider the manner in which Buell assimilated his materials and executed his design, we are on surer ground. If his map is to be considered as the work of a self-taught country engraver, not especially well educated and not trained in geographical observation, it must impress everyone who examines it as a *tour de force* that compels admiration. On any other grounds the production lays itself open to criticism. It is not drawn with the delicacy that we demand in maps; the lettering is in some areas crudely accomplished; the coast lines are freely conceived

Præses et Socii
Collegii Yalensis
Novo Portu Connecticutensium;
Omnibus has literas perlecturis Salutem in Domino. Notum sit
quod D. Stephanum Jacob Gradus Primi Candidatum, examine
usitato probatum, Præses, e Sociorum publicis Comitiis Assensu, Titulo,
Graduq Artium liberalium Baccalaurei, pro Meritis decoravit; et ei dedit
fruenda omnia Privilegia, Dignitates et Honores ad eundem Gradum, secundum
Jura Humanitatis, erga literatos ubique Terrarum pertinentia. Cujus
Sigillum Academiæ Nominaq nostra subscripta Testimonio sint.
Datum ex Ædibus academicis, Die Sept. 9no
Anno Salutis 1778vo
Annoq Reip: Amer: 3tio
Ezra Stiles S.T.D. Præses
Eliphalet Williams
Nathl Taylor
Moses Mather
Saml Lockwood
Timo Pitkin
Socii
A. Buell Sculp.

Diploma form engraved by Abel Buell, probably about 1774, for Yale College.

and coarsely executed, and in general there are apparent evidences of amateurishness and of haste. It is probable that the fear of being anticipated in publication by a rival cartographer drove him to hurried workmanship, the worst fault, ignorance excepted, that can beset a map engraver.

Buell's map of the United States then has little significance as a specimen of cartographical art, nor is its historical importance as great as we could wish it to be. He had been forestalled in showing the boundaries of the new political division by several English map makers whose works were published in 1783. "A Map of the United States of America as settled by the peace of 1783" appeared in *The European Magazine and London Review* soon after the Peace of 1783. Another English production, the John Wallis map, *The United States of America . . . Agreeable to the Peace of 1783. Published, April 3d 1783* has been described as "the first specially engraved map of the United States made after the Declaration of Peace." The Jefferys map in the *American Atlas* and the Faden map published in the year 1783 also showed these boundaries. The words "États Unis," possibly the first cartographical use of the new name, appeared on the J. B. Eliot *Carte du Théâtre de la Guerre,* of Paris, 1778, and several times afterwards in its English form before Buell employed it. Our engraver was doubtless aware of these facts when he made only the modest claim that his map of the United States was "the first ever compiled, engraved, and finished by one man, and an American." He seems to be entitled to this priority, at least, for although subscriptions were invited for William McMurray's "Map of the United States" in the *Pennsylvania Packet* of August 9, 1783, the production was not issued until December 17, 1784, nearly nine months later than the day on which Buell's map was declared ready for delivery.[74] A claim that one writer has made for him, that his map has on it "the first flag of the United States, published in a map by an American," seems to raise the question of what is and what is not significant in the concept of priority.

We may conclude the discussion of Buell's map with certain general observations. It has a peculiar local and personal interest; it is a landmark in the history of American engraving; and it has interest in the study of American cartography as the first map of the political division known as the United States of America to be compiled and engraved by one of its native-born citizens. That this map had some degree of local influence becomes apparent to one who examines in connection with it the small Amos Doolittle map of the United States of America that seems to have appeared first, unsigned, in Jedidiah Morse's *Geography Made Easy,* published in New Haven in the last week of December, 1784.[75] The same map, bearing the signature "A. Doolittle Sc.," was issued in New Haven late in 1785 in *An Astronomical Diary or Almanack, for 1786,* by Nathan Ben Salomon,[76] and the indications are that it was sold separately also in the intervening months. There are so many points of likeness between this small map and the large one before us that in comparing them one is assured of Doolittle's indebtedness to the map issued by his fellow townsman nine months before the appearance of the first Morse geography.

THE CONNECTICUT PENNIES

In our biographical chapter we wrote briefly of the mint conducted by Abel Buell and certain associates at different times in the period 1785 to 1789. An actual recording shows that in this period a constant change in details of the device, legends, and symbolism of the coin was in progress, many of them of the slightest consequence. The fact that some 350 variations have been counted suggests that others besides Buell had responsible access to the dies from which the coins were stamped. We can be reasonably sure, however, that the first of the coins issued in the beginning year of 1785 was of Buell's creation. It has been described as follows:[77]

Device or Obverse—A bust in coat of mail, head laureated, and facing to the right.
Legend—Auctori Connec.
Reverse—The Goddess of Liberty seated on the globe, facing to the left, the liberty pole, surmounted by the cap, in the left hand, and the olive branch in the right.
Legend—Inde:et Lib.
Dated—1785

This brings us to the end of our consideration of Buell as an engraver. In the course of it there have been described five plates: the Saybrook chart, the Yale diploma, *The Sequel of Arts and Sciences,* the arms of Connecticut, and the great map of the United States. To these must be added the dies for the Connecticut Pennies. The plates for the Romans Florida chart and other productions in which he may have assisted Romans must remain in doubt, but even without these, enough has been presented to give Abel Buell a decent rank among early American engravers. His great wall map of the United States, "compiled, engraved, and finished by one man," was at the time of its publication one of the most ambitious undertakings in the history of American engraving, and poor though the result was in some particulars the intention was of the highest order. He was the first Connecticut engraver, preceding Doolittle in point of time just as Doolittle later surpassed him in productivity and in excellence of workmanship; but, as we have seen, Buell's strength lay in his aptitude for the beginning of enterprises ultimately of great importance. We can afford to overlook a certain lack of finish in his undertakings.

Conclusion

IN bringing this narrative to an end, one feels the need of a summary statement of the results of Buell's life of activity. It is possible to form a list of achievements that is not without impressiveness, though some of the items in the list are naturally of small importance. Here follow the noteworthy results of his life of ingenious craftsmanship:

A lifetime of work as silversmith, jeweller, and lapidary.

The construction of a practicable lapidary's cutting and polishing machine.

The cutting and casting of the earliest font of roman letter known to be made in English America.

The engraving of Parker's Chart of Saybrook Bar, the first engraving of any consequence made in Connecticut.

The engraving, possibly, of some of the plates for Bernard Romans's Florida chart; the engraving of the Yale diploma, *The Sequel of Arts and Sciences,* the arms of the state, and, finally, the compilation and engraving of his great wall map of the United States.

The casting of type in sufficient quantity during the Revolution to enable certain Connecticut printers to carry on their publications more satisfactorily to themselves and to their readers.

The construction and operation of a machine for coining copper money and the designing and making of the necessary dies.

The construction of the second cotton mill in New Haven, said at the time to be the first built on successful lines.

The invention of a corn planting machine.

The construction of mechanical devices and of models and patterns and dies which must have been an important feature in the industrial beginnings of his state.

Through these achievements one sees Abel Buell as a craftsman who differed from most of his kind in that he never permitted the busy play of his hands to lull his mind to slumber. He brooded continually after the fashion of most manual laborers, but he put his dreams to the test of action. When he found the results lacking in the essential thing that makes for success, he turned at once to other schemes. And always with each of his projects, a bit of luck would have set him high. Had he been asked on his pauper's deathbed for an estimate of his career, I doubt that he would have admitted failure. One more chance would have been his last demand of life.

There is a final thing that needs to be said of Abel Buell. Silversmith, artist, engineer, inventor, pattern maker, die cutter, maker of agricultural implements, auctioneer, quarryman, shipowner, mill operator—all of these things he was that since his time have been the life of his state and of a large part of his nation. One sees him, therefore, as a symbol of the pioneer community in which he lived, the symbol of a people that replied to the demands of life with strokes from weapons forged sturdily in the life-giving fires of Necessity.

Notes

1. *The History of the Buell Family,* Compiled by Albert Welles, New York, 1881, pp. 118–19.

2. Barber, John Warner, *Connecticut Historical Collections,* New Haven, 1838, p. 531. See also Curtis, G. M., *Early Silver of Connecticut and its Makers,* pp. 53–57. In colonial America, the work of the goldsmith, generic name of the craftsman who worked in gold and silver, was carried out chiefly with the less precious metal as its basic material. Unless, therefore, the context seems to require the use of the comprehensive "goldsmith," we shall think and speak of Buell and his associates in the ancient craft as silversmiths.

3. The Parker surname is suggested, though not affirmed, in the Buell family history cited in note 1, above. The more convincing Chittenden origin of Mrs. Mary Buell is set forth in Alvin Talcott, *Genealogy of the Chittenden Family,* 1882, p. 21. The date of the marriage is arrived at by inference from an entry in the New Haven County Court Records, 5:493, January, 1763.

4. *Public Records of the Colony of Connecticut,* 12:288 and 379–80, give an account of the transfer some years before 1764 of certain real estate belonging to Buell. All circumstances considered, it seems unlikely that he could have acquired this property at so early an age otherwise than by inheritance.

5. The law under which Buell was tried and condemned had been on the books since the Assembly of May, 1724. Before that time the punishment for this offense had been only six months' imprisonment and treble damages to the injured persons. The later law provided the loss of the right ear, branding on the forehead, forfeiture of estate, and life imprisonment.

6\. *Public Records of the Colony of Connecticut,* 12:354, May, 1765. The details of the alteration are found in a newspaper notice (reported to me by Mr. Thompson Harlow, director of the Connecticut Historical Society) in the *New London Gazette,* April 6, 1764. John Warner Barber, in his richly stored work cited in note 2, above, says that the bills were raised by Buell from five shillings to five pounds. The contemporary report of the *New London Gazette* must be accepted as the more reliable in this detail.

7\. Barber, *Connecticut Historical Collections,* p. 531.

8\. *Virginia Gazette,* August 11, 1738.

9\. Stauffer, D. McN., *American Engravers upon Copper and Steel,* 1:61.

10\. *Ibid.,* 1:20, 33. The whole subject is broadly treated in a recent work, Kenneth Scott, *Counterfeiting in Colonial America,* New York, 1957.

11\. *Public Records of the Colony of Connecticut,* 12:288, May, 1764.

12\. Connecticut Archives, Crimes and Misdemeanors, 1663–1788, 5:244 and 245.

13\. *Public Records of the Colony of Connecticut,* 12:527, October, 1766.

14\. Rivington's successful application for a writ of attachment, its service by the constable, and his report upon the attached real estate and the articles in the house and shop, as related in the text, are found in the collection of papers described as "Superior Court, New Haven County, files on deposit, Connecticut State Library." I am indebted to Mr. Thompson Harlow for locating these documents and supplying me with photostats of them.

15\. Hildeburn, C. R., *Sketches of Printers and Printing in Colonial New York,* pp. 119–21, tells the story of the attack upon Rivington's shop. Copies of the satirical poem, tentatively attributed to Philip Freneau by Victor Hugo Paltsits in *A Bibliography of the . . . Works of Philip Freneau,* pp. 25–27, are found in the New York Public Library and the John Carter Brown Library.

16. For an interesting account of this unhappy enterprise by one of its leading participants, see *The Memoirs of Rufus Putnam,* edited by Rowena Buell, Boston, 1903, pp. 36–54.

17. The Samuel Shethar memorial is found in "Connecticut Archives, Manuscript Index, Revolutionary War, 1763–1789. Series 1, vol. 23, Doc. 156, pages a–g," Connecticut State Library. Knowledge of the memorial was communicated by Mr. Thompson R. Harlow, Librarian of the Connecticut Historical Society. A photostat was courteously supplied by the Connecticut State Library.

17a. Work cited in note 2, above, page 532.

18. Connecticut Archives, Finance and Currency, 1677–1789, 5:161a.

19. Hamilton, F. W., *Types and Presses in America,* Chicago, 1918.

20. New Haven County Court Records, 8:407, December, 1779. James Rivington, plaintiff vs. Abel Buell, defendant, in an action of Book Debt for £500 continued from April, 1775: Defendant appeared but plaintiff appeared not and court awarded defendant costs.

21. Middlebrook, L. F., *History of Maritime Connecticut during the American War,* 2 v., Salem, 1925, 2:173.

22. Buell has caused his biographer no little perplexity about his wives—their names and their number. Here is the tale:

On the basis of a document citing Abel Buell and his wife before the New Haven County Court (Records, vol. 5, p. 498, January, 1763), it is known that the name of the first wife was Mary and that they were married late in the year 1762. On the authority of Albert Welles, *The History of the Buell Family,* it is suggested that the surname of this wife was Parker, but on this point see the discussion in our text and our conclusion that she was Mary Chittenden. On September 21, 1770, the *Connecticut Journal* of New Haven contained the following notice: "Last Sunday departed this life, in the XXVIIIth year of her age, Mrs. Mary Buell, the amiable consort of Mr. Abel Buell, of this town." The issue of this union seems to be unknown, but in 1789 Buell went to England and left with his son Benjamin authority to continue the operation of the machine for coining coppers. As this machine represented the semi-official mint of the state, it is not likely that such authority would have been left with a minor. We may assume that this Benjamin was the son of Abel and Mary Buell.

Buell next married Aletta, or Letty, whose maiden name is given as Devoe in the family history mentioned above. This marriage occurred probably sometime in the year 1771, for on October 15, 1772, was buried their daughter, Deborah (Trinity Church records, New Haven). A son, Abel, was baptized February 5, 1773, and died February 16, 1773. I have found no other references to children by this wife. Aletta is last heard of in September, 1777.

Now comes matter that may be debatable. One Abel Buell of New Haven married about the year 1779 Rebecca (Parkman) Townsend (born December 14, 1751, died December, 1800). The children by this marriage were Henry Parkman, baptized June 4, 1780; Rebecca, born in October, 1781, and died April 14, 1782; Abel, baptized March 6, 1785; Jeremiah, baptized February 8, 1789 (Center Church records).

For the reason that it is nowhere mentioned that this Abel Buell of New Haven who married Rebecca Townsend was our Abel Buell, silversmith of New Haven, there might exist in the minds of some a doubt of this identity. But the probability is high that these were the same man. Our Abel would have been at this time only thirty-seven years of age, marrying a woman of twenty-eight years. To the general probability must be added the fact that in preparing this study no other person named Abel Buell encountered in New Haven newspapers and records seems to fit the circumstances as well as our subject.

The Federal Census of 1790 for Connecticut gives only one Abel Buell in the index and he is our man without a doubt, living in New Haven near or next door to Ebenezer Chittenden. It is not likely that in this matter of the wives he could have become confused with the Abel Bewel of Lebanon who is recorded in the census. The census credits the New

Haven Abel Buell with having in his family three free white males under sixteen and two free white females, ages not specified. This is close to the number of inmates his house would have had if the above suppositions are correct. The son Benjamin, probably of Mary, was certainly over sixteen; there were no children remaining by Aletta and there were living three sons by Rebecca under sixteen. One of the two free white females would have been his wife, Rebecca; the other is unknown. We know also that Abel Buell, the New Haven silversmith, moved to Hartford about 1799, and that in 1803 he transferred by deed dated East Hartford, August 19, 1803, to Abel Buell, Jr., and to Margaret his wife, a lot in the new burial ground in New Haven adjoining that of Mr. John Townsend. The next entry (New Haven Land Records, vol. 57, p. 362) is a conveyance from Abel Buell of the City of New York, Mariner, and Margaret his wife, of the same lot to William B. Townsend also of New York. Now we have here a person who seems to be our Abel Buell of New Haven and Hartford conveying a lot to his son Abel Buell, Jr., of New York, who transfers it to a William B. Townsend of New York. This in all probability was the same Abel Buell who some twenty-four years earlier had married a Rebecca Townsend and a few years afterward had by her a son named Abel.

Rebecca, the third wife of Abel, died sometime in December, 1800, and, assuming that we are meeting with only one Abel, he married for the fourth time and soon afterwards became a widower again. The *Connecticut Courant* of Hartford, August 31, 1803, gives us this death notice: "In this City, Mrs. Sally Buell, wife of Mr. Abel Buell, aged 34 years." The Hartford Sexton's list gives the date of burial as August 29, 1803. Whether the bereaved husband attempted a fifth trial at matrimony, I have not discovered.

23. Middlebrook, work cited in note 21, 2:233.

24. New Haven Land Records, 41:160.

25. In his *Early Silver of Connecticut and its Makers,* pp. 54, 55, George Munson Curtis discussed the location of Buell's shop, "The Sign of the Coffee Pot," and the land upon which

it stood with relation to the properties of Robert Fairchild and Ebenezer Chittenden. Reference as to this matter of location may also be made to New Haven Land Records, 41:160, 43:349, 46:26, and 46:135.

26. The story of this company that follows is taken from the report of the Assembly committee appointed in January, 1789, to inquire into the conduct of the coinage scheme. The report was dated April 2, 1789, and is found in the Connecticut State Library, Connecticut Archives, Manuscript Index, Miscellaneous, 1662–1789, 3:251a, b, c. The original resolution of October, 1785, authorizing the private mint is found in *Public Records of the State of Connecticut,* 1785–1789, Vol. VI, pages 121–122. For other references see our note 77, below.

27. New Haven Land Records, 43:349, January 21, 1789.

28. New Haven Land Records, 46:26.

29. Dexter, F. B., ed., *Literary Diary of Ezra Stiles,* 3:562.

30. New Haven Land Records, 57:362.

31. Jones, E. F., *Stockbridge, Past and Present,* pp. 264–66; and Field, D. D., *An Historical Sketch, Congregational, of the Church in Stockbridge, Massachusetts,* 1853, p. 26. It was probably an echo of Buell's reputed atheism that led to the attribution to him (see Moore, John W., *Historical Notes on Printing,* Concord, 1886, p. 19) of a weekly newspaper, *The Devil's Club or Iron Cane.* Mr. Clarence Brigham, final authority in the field of American newspapers, communicated this information to me with the comment that he had not been able to locate a publication of that title. The only book known to me as having belonged to Buell is a copy (John Carter Brown Library) of a Revolutionary political pamphlet entitled *A Brief Review of the Rise, Progress, Services and Sufferings of New-England,* Norwich, 1774. Inscribed upon the title page is "Abel Buell His Book." This single title, of course, is meaningless with respect to Buell's reading or his religious belief.

32. Similar entries are in the *National Pilot,* March 21, 1822, and in the *Connecticut Herald* for March 26, 1822. See also the published New Haven Vital Records, p. 604, where is recorded this death under the Second Congregational Society.

33. Barber, *Connecticut Historical Collections,* p. 531.

34. Dexter, F. B., *Itineraries of Ezra Stiles,* p. 463.

35. See note 14, above.

35a. I express thanks to Messrs. Paul Benson and Carl Stickney of the Brown University Department of Buildings and Grounds for knowledge of the cooper's plane which, at Mr. Benson's suggestion, was brought to me by its owner, Mr. Stickney, who is interested in the history and antiquities of the carpenter's craft.

36. These pieces are entered and described and the maker's mark displayed in Jones, E. Alfred, *The Old Silver of American Churches,* p. 357. A photograph of the cups is reproduced, plate xxix, in Mr. Curtis's *Early Silver of Connecticut.* As related, two of the cups are in Mr. Hammerslough's collection, one in the collection of Mr. Robert Graham, of New York, and the fourth at Yale.

37. *Public Records of the Colony of Connecticut,* 13:518, October, 1771, and 14:95, May, 1773.

38. Dexter, *Itineraries of Ezra Stiles,* p. 476. The "American Society" was the American Philosophical Society of which both Gale and Stiles were members.

39. *Ibid.,* pp. 494–95.

40. From the unpublished portion of the Stiles Papers in the possession of Yale University.

41. Dexter, *Itineraries of Ezra Stiles,* pp. 448, 449, 449n.

42. *Early Proceedings of the American Philosophical Society,* Philadelphia, 1884, pp. 36, 39, 41.

43. A claim to priority in the production of type in a given community must rest, after all, upon an actual specimen of type or upon unquestionable documentary evidence. No acceptable specimen has yet been brought forward in support of the assertion made in David Mitchelson's behalf by the writer in the *Massachusetts Gazette,* quoted in the text. The only suggestion known to me ever made in this connection is the so-called *Boston Chronicle* type employed by John Mein, the Boston publisher, in various publications after 1766. This suggestion has been made because the type face in question is unlike any other

of the place and period and because an association of some sort almost certainly existed between Mein and Mitchelson. The question was discussed by me in an appendix to the first edition of the present work. In my book, *The Colonial Printer* (2d ed., 1938, facing p. 102), I reproduced the broadside display or specimen sheet, showing this type face, issued by Mein & Fleeming late in 1766 or early in 1767. But my own imperfect and inconclusive discussions of the subject have been superseded by the researches and acute interpretations made by Mr. John Alden of the Boston Public Library, embodied in a series of articles culminating in his "Scotch Type in Eighteenth-Century America," published in *Studies in Bibliography, Papers of the Bibliographical Society of the University of Virginia,* Vol. III (1950–51), pp. 270–74. In this article, the correctness of Isaiah Thomas's assertion (*History of Printing in America,* 1st ed., 1810, II:46) that the *Boston Chronicle* type had been imported from an Edinburgh foundry is demonstrated so tellingly as to leave very little room for dissent. Unless other evidence becomes available, the Mitchelson claim may very well be left as an interesting, not improbable, but unproven assertion of success.

44. Connecticut Archives, Industry, 2:137.

45. *Ibid.,* 2:138.

46. *Ibid.,* 2:139, whence it has been reprinted in *Public Records of the Colony of Connecticut,* 13:273, October, 1769.

47. *Ibid.,* 2:158.

48. *Public Records of the State of Connecticut,* 1:381, August, 1777.

49. See note 18, above.

50. Trumbull, No. 78, says that this almanac was probably printed by Timothy Green of New London.

51. There is a copy of this sermon in the John Carter Brown Library.

52. Barber, *Connecticut Historical Collections,* p. 532.

53. Thomas, Isaiah, *History of Printing in America,* 2d ed., I:27.

54. See Wroth, Lawrence C., "The First Work with Ameri-

can Types," *Bibliographical Essays, A Tribute to Wilberforce Eames,* New York, 1924, pp. 128–42.

55. *Public Records of the Colony of Connecticut,* 12:383.

56. *Ibid.,* 13:643.

57. Connecticut Archives, Lotteries and Divorces, 1755–1789, 1:93. For Parker's Memorial see same, 1:91.

58. Connecticut Archives, Lotteries and Divorces, 1755–1789, 1:92.

59. Connecticut Archives, Lotteries and Divorces, 1755–1789, 1:155.

60. E. Harold Hugo and Thompson R. Harlow. *Abel Buell a Jack of all trades, & Genius Extraordinary . . . Illustrated by . . . a Chart and a Writing Sheet . . . made from the original copies in the Collection of The Connecticut Historical Society* . . . (Meriden, Connecticut, MDCCCCLV). The "Chart of Saybrook Barr" is reproduced in this extremely handsome production and is discussed on page [6]. The writing sheet, or to give it its title, *The Sequel of Arts and Sciences,* inserted in an accompanying folder, is beautifully reproduced in collotype in full size and in the colors of the copy in the Connecticut Historical Society. This publication does honor to its authors and to its sponsor, The Columbiad Club, which issued it as its Keepsake Number 56.

61. *Ibid.,* pp. [6, 7].

62. Barber, *Connecticut Historical Collections,* p. 532. See also Stauffer, *American Engravers upon Copper and Steel,* I:35.

63. See p. 30 and pp. 45–51 of Phillips, P. Lee, *Notes on the Life and Works of Bernard Romans,* Deland, Florida, 1924. (Publications of the Florida State Historical Society, No. 2.)

64. These points are brought out in the letters between Dr. Lorimer and Romans that Mr. Phillips has included, pp. 27–30, in the work cited in the preceding note.

65. *Ibid.,* p. 24.

66. *Ibid.,* p. 50.

67. *Ibid.,* p. 25.

68. It must be said that in his superb book, *Paul Revere's Engravings,* Mr. Clarence S. Brigham affirms his belief that

Revere was responsible for the engraving not only of the three plates for the Florida charts charged in his account books but for the whole series of nine plates which made up the great Romans production. His argument in substantiation is as rich in assumptions and individual interpretations as that which I have here set forth in behalf of Abel Buell's possible participation in that important work. Mr. Brigham is on solid ground, of course, in affirming the existence of a Romans-Rivington-Revere business relationship, and in his observation of uniformity in style of lettering throughout the nine plates of the Florida charts. It is clear from our text, however, that there existed also a Romans-Rivington-Buell business relationship. It can be said, furthermore, that many of the letter forms employed on the Florida charts are very close in style to certain of those found on Buell's *Map of the United States* of 1784. In view of this balancing of fact and assumption, Mr. Brigham and I are well agreed that a final decision as to who engraved what for the Florida charts must await documentation.

69. Work cited in note 63, above, pp. 38–39, where Mr. Phillips puts forward his view that Rivington was not the printer of Romans's *Concise Natural History of East and West Florida.* In *Paul Revere's Engravings,* pp. 93–94, Mr. Brigham presents an argument to the contrary which seems more cogent than Mr. Phillips's denial. It may be added to the evidence they adduce that on February 3, 1774 (see Phillips, *Bernard Romans,* pp. 27–28), Romans referred to Mr. Rivington and Mr. Hazard as the only persons on earth who with his knowledge had up to that time seen any part of his manuscript. That statement seems to bring Rivington close to the work.

70. Phillips, *Bernard Romans,* p. 92, from the *Connecticut Courant,* January 5 and 19, 1779. See also *Connecticut Journal,* March 3, 1779.

71. Connecticut Archives, Finance and Currency, 1677–1789, 5:213a.

72. Bates, *Connecticut Statute Laws,* Nos. 249 and 250, and p. 6. The likeness between the cuts is so exact in every detail, except in the areas specified, that the process of re-engraving

may hardly be considered as having been employed for their duplication. In his advertisement of May 18, 1796, we find Buell advertising his ability to provide "casting moulds" and "patterns and models of any sort of cast work." He had, of course, become familiar with casting procedures in his work as silversmith and type founder.

73. L. C. Karpinski in the *Dearborn Independent* for October 24, 1925. Admirable reproductions of the Hutchins book and map, supplemented by valuable biographical and bibliographical materials, form the contents of *Thomas Hutchins. A Topographical Description of Virginia. . . .* Edited by Frederick Charles Hicks. Cleveland, 1904.

74. Phillips, *Bernard Romans,* p. 33.

75. Evans, *American Bibliography,* No. 18615.

76. Bates, *Check List of Connecticut Almanacs,* p. 49.

77. The general historical aspects of the Company for Coining Coppers as treated in this study are found in the original documents referred to in our note 26, above; in the note by Leonard Woods Labaree, page 121, *Public Records of the State of Connecticut,* Vol. VI; and in Bronson, Henry, "A Historical Account of Connecticut Currency. . . ," separately paged iv, 1–192, in *Papers of the New Haven Colony Historical Society,* Vol. I, New Haven, 1865, specifically pages 176–181. The numismatic aspect is admirably treated in Dickeson, M. W., *The American Numismatic Manual,* Philadelphia, 1865, pages 102–112, and "Supplement," pages 258–261, where a great number of varieties of the penny for the years 1785–1788 are listed and differentiated, and where, Plate X, certain of them are illustrated in color. Our description of the coin of 1785 is adapted from Dickeson, page 102.

Index

Index

Index

Abel Buell

OF CONNECTICUT

has been composed in Linotype Baskerville and printed from type by Connecticut Printers, Incorporated, of Hartford. The illustrations, reproduced from original documents, have been printed by offset by the Meriden Gravure Company. The paper is Mead's Suede Book, laid; the binding cloth is Holliston's Aldine. Binding is by the Russell-Rutter Company.

Wesleyan University Press

MIDDLETOWN, CONNECTICUT